China, American Catholicism,
and the Missionary

CHINA,
AMERICAN CATHOLICISM,
AND THE MISSIONARY

Thomas A. Breslin

The Pennsylvania State University Press
University Park and London

Library of Congress Cataloging in Publication Data

Breslin, Thomas A
  China, American Catholicism, and the missionary.
  Includes bibliography and index.
  1. Missions—China. 2. Catholic Church—Missions.
3. Missions, American. I. Title.
BV3415.2.B74   266'.251   79-27857
ISBN 0-271-00259-X

To the memory of my father, Joseph P. Breslin,
and for my mother, Agnes T. Breslin

Contents

Maps

Preface

Until a few years ago, the missionary was the "hidden" person in American foreign relations.[1] The most ambitious recent endeavor in the study of American-East Asian relations was a symposium convened at Cuernavaca, Mexico, in 1972 to explore the role of American Protestant missionaries in China. The collection of essays which resulted from the conference ended with a decidedly anti-missionary diatribe by Arthur M. Schlesinger, Jr., who saw in the missionaries and their enterprise the most dangerous and harmful aspect of the West's behavior toward China during the nineteenth and twentieth centuries.[2] Articles since the symposium have depicted the China missionaries either as partners in the semicolonization of China or as a potential nexus between the West and the Communist regime which seized power in 1949.[3]

With few exceptions, historians have concentrated on the activities and significance of American Protestant missionaries while neglecting the activities of Roman Catholics. Linguistic and cultural barriers as well as the geographic dispersion of the archival sources may explain some of this unwarranted neglect. Yet the genesis of Roman Catholic missionary activity, the nature of the Catholic groups, and their relationship to the Chinese and to the foreign powers raise important historical questions.

While seeking answers to those questions, I studied the archives of a dozen missionary groups and pertinent U.S. Department of State records. The research yielded evidence that twentieth-century American Catholic missions to China were in part a reaction to American nativism and European disdain and in part a result of Vatican concern for the future of the Catholic Church in China. The evidence indicated that, rather than being an insidious danger to the Chinese, the missions' introduction of novelty, their generally benevolent parasitism, their blatantly opulent and privileged mode of operation, and their tempting weakness contributed to the resurgence of Chinese nationalism and to the downfall of foreign power in twentieth-century China.

The Pinyin system of spelling Chinese words is used in this book. On January 1, 1979, the People's Republic of China began using the Pinyin system in press dispatches. Subsequently, leading United States newspapers, the United Nations, and the United States Board on Geographic Names, which determines the official American spelling of place names, adopted the Pinyin system. Pinyin thus replaced the so-called conventional forms or Post Office spellings and the Wade-Giles transcription system used by academics in the United States. To assist the reader, the conventional or the Wade-Giles transcription of important names familiar to American readers at the time of the changeover is given in parentheses after the Pinyin version.

This groundbreaking work owes much to the hospitality generously extended to me by many missionary groups, especially by the Jesuits, the Maryknoll Fathers, the Passionist Fathers and the Vincentian Fathers, by many active and retired missionaries, and by my fellow academicians. I wish to express my gratitude for that hospitality as well as for the helpful criticisms, suggestions, and information offered to me by many individuals, especially William J. Duiker and Paul Varg. A travel fellowship from the American-East Asian Relations Committee of the American Historical Association made possible research and additional Chinese language study in Taiwan and Hong Kong. A grant from the Florida International University Foundation offset some of the publication costs of this book.

Melanie Samuelson helped to type earlier drafts of this work. Ana Amador and Isabel Barzana assisted with the typing of the final draft.

John M. Pickering, Carole Schwager, and their colleagues at The Pennsylvania State University Press were of great assistance in preparing the manuscript for publication.

Four persons, Norman A. Graebner, John Israel, William T. Olson, and Maida Watson-Espener, were especially helpful and encouraging and to them I am especially grateful.

Introduction

There was little room for organized religion in traditional Chinese society. The state and its clients generally preferred to monopolize the surplus generated by the peasantry rather than allow scarce resources to be diverted to the support of church structures. The powerful developed, as part of their Confucian ideology, political rituals with a religious dimension designed to instill awe and obedience in the peasantry, and to exude a confidence that the political order was linked to the unseen forces which ruled the visible world. In the Confucian scheme of things, the emperor was the pivot between earth and cosmos. But the official religious practice was too distant and rarified to ameliorate the uncertainties and losses of everyday life. Consequently there emerged in China, as C. K. Yang has written, "a vast number of magical practices and beliefs; the average man's mental picture of the universe—in fact, the whole pattern of his life—was heavily colored by a shadowy world of gods, spirits, and specters."[1]

When disaster overwhelmed China and its social order began to disintegrate, as at the end of the later Han dynasty, organized, formal religion was able to enter China or to take shape from local cults. Thus Buddhism entered China: in a period of political disorganization, it spread and flourished with invading tribes, and, after several centuries of growth in size and wealth, withered when the Tang dynasty turned against it and strengthened the traditional social and political order. During the same period Daoism emerged as an organized mass religion and provided an ideology for anti-Han rebels. Although the Daoists eventually made their peace with the Chinese state, Daoist sects would continue to stage occasional political upheavals, thereby reinforcing Confucian suspicions of organized religion. By the time Christianity reached China, organized religion was firmly identified as an ideological vehicle for rebels or invaders and as a competitor for scarce resources.

Christianity Arrives in China

Christianity first appeared in China during the seventh century, as a religion identified with the border tribes which separated China from rampaging Muslims. After the death of Mohammed, the Muslims swept out of Arabia and conquered the Syriac provinces of the Byzantine Empire. They drove before them many Christians who sought refuge in the Chinese

Empire, often among the border tribes employed by the Tang dynasty to contain the Arabs. Nestorian Christianity, as the Mesopotamian variety was called, did not spread to the Chinese because the Chinese saw the border tribes as powerful enemies. Residents professing the same faiths as the nomads were suspect; in 845, when the Emperor Wu Cung suppressed Buddhism and Manicheanism, he also suppressed and destroyed the Christianity in China.

Nestorian Christianity returned to China in the early thirteenth century, when Christian subjects of Kublai Khan, the Mongol conqueror, helped to overthrow the reigning Sung dynasty. The Nestorians, however, made few converts among the Chinese and Christianity again passed from the scene when the Chinese under the Ming turned the Mongols out in 1368.

Early Roman Catholic Missions to China

The Roman Christian presence in China under Mongol rule was equally transitory. Western Christendom had been terrorized when the victorious Mongol horde appeared on the European borderlands in the mid-thirteenth century. After a bloody crusade against the Albigensian heretics and still bothered by the Waldensian heresy, the Christians of Western Europe found the new threat all the more horrible. So Pope Innocent IV dispatched members of the Franciscan Order to turn aside the invaders or convert them. Later, missions composed of Franciscans or members of the Order of Preachers (Dominicans) reached as far as the Mongol capital at Karakorum in Central Asia. Shortly after Kublai Khan died in 1294 a Franciscan priest, John of Montecorvino, reached Cambulac (Beijing), the Mongol capital of China. Despite opposition from the Nestorians, John found favor with the emperor and began to proselytize. More friars traveled to China, established Franciscan houses, and worked among the Mongols and their allies rather than among the Chinese. With the victory of the antiforeign Ming and the end of Mongol rule in China, Roman Christianity, like Nestorian Christianity, disappeared.

More than 200 years would pass before Christian missionaries would return to China. In the interim the Roman Catholic Church was beset by theological and philosophical dissent and the claims of secular leaders to authority over the Church in their realms. One result was a cleavage in Christendom. Northwestern Europe broke away from Rome, the "Whore of Babylon," and its Mediterranean culture in a movement known as the Reformation. This shock was all the more grave because the Muslims remained a serious threat on the southern and eastern rim of the Mediterranean. The Vatican responded by using the newly founded Society of Jesus to restore discipline to the Church, counteract the Reformation, and conduct missionary ventures in South and East Asia. The Jesuits' activities in Europe stabilized the Roman Church and the reports of their worldwide missionary work restored the confidence of Roman Catholics.

Jesuit activity in China was aimed at the conversion of the Chinese court, and through it, the conversion of the entire Chinese society. Opponents of the Jesuits' strategy seized upon the Jesuits' acceptance of the Confucian order of things and joined with the Jansenists, the Calvinist branch of Roman Catholicism, to turn the Vatican against the Jesuits. Fearful that the Jesuits were encouraging the Chinese emperor to dictate the circumstances under which Catholicism could operate in China, the Vatican announced to the Emperor that it reserved to itself full authority over Catholicism in China. Consequently, Catholicism fell from favor and was proscribed in China. The Jesuit Order, beset by grasping monarchs and bitter rivals, fell from Rome's favor and was dissolved for forty years before being reconstituted in the early nineteenth century.

The task of reinforcing the foreign missionary presence in China now fell mainly on the Congregation of the Mission, a society of secular priests founded in 1625 by Vincent de Paul. Yet until 1830, fewer than twenty Vincentians had reached China. The Church had entered into an age of political and social revolution in Europe. Opposed by the revolutionary governments of France, the Church lost temporarily the means and the personnel to maintain a large missionary effort. The French government would again support French Catholic missions, but as the decades went by churchmen experienced a more profound crisis, the defection of the growing urban population of Europe.[2] The Roman church reacted by taking its faith for peasants overseas in search of other peasants to convert. This renewed missionary impulse accelerated in the late 1830s and continued into the twentieth century.[3]

1

The Return of the Christian Missions
to Qing China

At the end of the eighteenth century China seemed to be a world power. One hundred years later it was a backward nation at the mercy of the technologically advanced Western nations. With military support, thousands of Western businessmen and missionaries ranged across the land creating and catering to a taste for novel ideas and products. In the process they buttressed a multinational capitalist hegemony over China. But both merchants and missionaries introduced changes which undermined capitalist influence. After several turbulent decades, foreign hegemony in China collapsed, foreign troops and gunboats withdrew, and missionaries and merchants followed in their wake.

The Opening of Qing China

After a generation of struggle against France, Britain began to extend its newly won world power beyond India into Southeast Asia. Great Britain employed its naval force to carry back to England from Asia, Africa, and the Americas the capital needed to propel the industrial revolution, the sugar used to soothe and the tea to energize the new proletariate. Through the tightly regulated port of Guangzhou (Canton), China supplied the addicted West with tea as well as silk, cotton cloth, and porcelain.

Blessed with a vast and varied internal market, the Chinese had no use for Western products and continued to demand silver in payment for exports. The British and their American cousins who shared the China trade found it increasingly difficult to obtain enough silver to satisfy the Western craving for tea. So they smuggled into China another addictive plant, opium, a product both cultivated and imported by the Chinese despite an imperial ban near the end of the eighteenth century.

If any nations in 1820 could have absorbed the cost of widespread opium addiction, China was initially one of them. Its enormous population, about 350,000,000, was rapidly increasing. The economy was self-sufficient, the result of foreign silver flowing in over the preceding decades. Its formal government network of civilian and military authority seemed to have the country firmly under control, and at the grassroots level an extensive network of local Confucian-influenced officials supplemented the formal government. But the government's very successes and the country's economic prosperity had softened the bureaucrats and merchants, leaving them free to indulge in the delights of the opium pipe. Consumption of smuggled opium increased sharply after 1820, despite the government's anti-opium campaigns.

The addiction of officials and their corruption by smugglers' bribes undermined Chinese government throughout southern China. Government efficiency declined, as did the momentum of business at the very time agrarian unrest was appearing in many parts of China. Secret societies were at the core of many uprisings among the Chinese; ethnic minorities formed the resistance in the other cases. The government made fitful attempts to ban opium and managed to crush the uprisings but it had no solutions for the failure of agricultural production to keep pace with the population growth. In the face of these staggering problems, many officials sought refuge in opium or dilettantism.

The British and American merchants were eager to supply the Chinese opium habit. In fact, only through the sale of opium could the Westerners support their caffeine addiction. In 1836, the British imported $17,000,000 worth of Chinese tea and silk and sold $18,000,000 worth of opium.[1] The trade had become so important to the British that in 1834 the government sent an official representative to head up the British presence. This appointment came shortly before a concerted effort by the Chinese government to suppress the opium trade once and for all. This effort, headed by the special commissioner Lin Zexu, led to the collapse of the opium trade and British military intervention.

From its outbreak in November 1839, until hostilities ended with the Treaty of Nanjing in August 1842, the First Opium War was one-sided. The British expeditionary force to China easily defeated the technologically backward Manchu troops and Chinese militia who opposed them. Under the terms of the treaty the Chinese were made to pay an indemnity of $21,000,000, abolish their restrictive trade system, open Shanghai, Guangzhou, and three other South China ports to the British, cede Hong Kong, recognize Great Britain as an equal, and promise to establish quickly a fixed tariff. The supplementary Treaty of the Bogue gave Britain most favored nation status. Subsequent negotiations gave similar rights to the French and Americans. The Treaty of Nanjing also gave legal sanction to Protestant missionary activity in the treaty ports; an 1844 imperial edict granted toleration to Chinese Catholics.

Relations between China and the West were often strained in the years that followed the First Opium War, in part from Chinese slowness in opening the designated treaty ports and in part from Western insistence on continuing the opium trade. Relations were also strained because Roman Catholic missionaries worked illegally in the interior, beyond the treaty ports, and because Protestant missionaries became involved with the Hakka Chinese who blended Christianity into an anti-Confucian ideology and staged a nearly successful rebellion from 1850 to 1864. That rebellion was caused by natural disasters and the economic dislocation resulting from the importation of opium and foreign manufactures.

These tensions culminated in the Second Opium War. Fighting broke out between Chinese and foreign forces near Guangzhou in late 1856. Although an American frigate briefly entered the fray against the Chinese, the British found their main support in the French, who were seeking revenge for the official execution of a French missionary priest. The foreign troops took Guangzhou in 1857; when they threatened Beijing (Peking) in 1858, the Chinese sued for peace.

The treaty of 1858 designated ten more treaty ports and opened the interior to foreigners, including missionaries. By its terms, Chinese Christians were free to practice their religion and the foreign signatory powers stationed representatives in Beijing and were accorded indemnities for the war. Difficulties developed during the ratification ceremonies and in 1860 the British and French fought their way to Beijing and looted and burned the imperial summer palace. Under the disputed terms of the subsequent agreement with the French government, French missionaries (or those holding French passports, as many Catholics of other nationalities were to do) were free to rent or buy land anywhere in the Chinese empire and to erect buildings on that land.

English and American Protestant Missions to China

Like the European Catholic missionaries, the English and American Protestant missionaries who appeared in China from 1829 represented churches that were experiencing profound difficulties at home. The secular regime in France and the propaganda of its supporters such as Tom Paine had shocked Christianity in England. This external phenomenon, which in its own way initially seemed as threatening as the Mongols and Muslims had to Christians of an earlier age, paralleled a more significant internal threat, the alienation of the swelling urban industrial proletariat. While religious enthusiasts sought to convert the unchurched at home, others sought out non-Christians in the Mideast, Ceylon, India, and, finally, East Asia.

In the United States, Protestants saw a secular national government and state after state break official ties with established churches. During this "Age of Paine," internal differences tore the churches. Ambitious laity, desiring the prestige of local church leadership and intent on perfecting society along Protestant Christian lines, organized national benevolent reform societies. These groups clashed with the slaveholding class, which opposed reformers' efforts to teach slaves to read anything, including the Bible. A great effort in the mid-1830s to reform the southwestern and western frontier areas was also unsuccessful. Subsequently, the Panic of 1837 dealt the national benevolent reform societies a staggering financial blow, upsetting their national aims.

The external threat came by boatloads: illiterate Irish who were staunch papists and antagonists of Protestant Christianity jammed the cities, performing brutally hard and dangerous work for a pittance. The Irish were the first wave of a huge European Catholic migration to America.

As the Catholics came in ever greater numbers, the American Protestant missionaries sailed off to the Mideast, to South Asia, and to East Asia in ever greater numbers. Protestants who remained at home sought less to convert the newcomers than to protect their own heritage from them.

In China the Protestant missionaries concentrated on education and medical work in the treaty ports. Their efforts in these fields increased Chinese knowledge of Western technology and skills. The Protestant religious message, with its stress on the individual, posed a direct challenge to the Confucian order, as the Taiping rebels demonstrated when they absorbed some Protestant Christian teachings into their ideology. This identification of Christianity with both foreign invaders and indigenous rebels reinforced the Confucian suspicion of organized religion.

Catholic Missionaries Launch a Counterreformation

Although many Catholic missionaries lived and proselytized in the treaty ports, Catholic missionaries worked in the interior of the country more than did the Protestants. Furthermore, unlike the Protestants, the Catholics were building upon a native base of tens of thousands of Chinese who traced their religious heritage to the seventeenth- and eighteenth-century Jesuits. These Chinese had maintained their Catholicism despite official persecution and lack of contact with priests, although a few foreign and Chinese priests had paid clandestine visits to the two Catholic Chinese areas: Beijing in the north and Shanghai and Nanjing in the south, an area known as Jiangnan.

In Jiangnan the Chinese Catholics had devised a distinctive form of local church government which would pose a major problem for the missionaries. The newcomers found that clan leaders and women played a prominent role in the Chinese Catholic style of church governance and that priests served a merely subsidiary function. Clan leaders managed all church lands and funds and arranged the priests' clandestine visits to their communities. They also maintained contact with the outside world and bought off otherwise trouble-some officials. Christian women, especially the single women known as "virgins," who dedicated themselves to church work, had great influence and power in their communities. From 1800 to 1850, for example, the leader of the Nanjing Christian community was a widow, He Daguan. The virgins cared for the chapels, many of which they themselves had built, undertook the religious instruction of Christian children, led the prayers at Mass and other services, and supported itinerant clergymen, including the Jesuits.[2] The virgins, who were quite numerous, lived with their families or in small, self-supporting groups, often adopting young girls to carry on their work. It was against these women especially that the Jesuits, who had returned to China in 1842, battled for control of the Catholic Church in Jiangnan.[3] Upon the outcome of that conflict hung the fate of Chinese Catholicism. A victory for the Jesuits would mean the reinstitution of Roman Catholicism. In the exact sense of the word, the Jesuits were promoting a counterreformation.

Ironically, the first Jesuits of the restored Society of Jesus went to China at the request of the laity and of the Administrator (later bishop) of the Nanjing diocese, Monsignor Louis-Marie de Besi. The Chinese laity remembered glorious tales of the Jesuits of old, before Pope Clement XIV suppressed the Society of Jesus in 1773. De Besi felt that the Vincentian, Franciscan, and Italian and Chinese secular (diocesan) priests in his diocese were too few; in answer to his request for assistance, the leadership of the Society of Jesus dispatched men to China.

The newly arrived Jesuits gave themselves over to pastoral work in Jiangnan. As they increased in number, Monsignor de Besi took the oppor-tunity to expel from his diocese the Vincentians, a group with which he had been feuding. Then he embarked on a fateful course. Disregarding the Jesuits' institutional ties, believing each priest should keep the rules of his society in his heart only, de Besi attempted to control all the clergy under him, and to receive and transmit all monies given by European Catholics for Jesuits in China. "The Jesuits have not come to Jiangnan as Jesuits but as missionaries," de Besi stated. The Jesuits countered that obedience to their own superiors was of the essence of their community. "A Jesuit is a Jesuit before being a missionary," wrote the head of the Jesuits' Province of Paris. He believed that the only solution was a Jesuit bishop of Nanjing.[4]

The Jesuits achieved the first step toward their goal of ecclesiastical domination in Jiangnan in 1856 when Rome suppressed the diocese of Nanjing and divided it into vicariates apostolic, ecclesiastical units closely controlled by Rome and headed by bishops who technically were personal representatives of the Pope. The Jesuits took over the area round Nanjing and Shanghai which until 1921 was known as the Vicariate Apostolic of

Jiangnan. Once having gained full ecclesiastical powers in their area, the Jesuits ordered the Chinese secular priests to live in Jesuit houses as subjects of the full Jesuit discipline.[5]

The next steps were more difficult. The priests had to regain control of the church properties, many but not all of which had once been owned by the presuppression Society of Jesus. They also had to assert control of the local churches, which meant stripping both the clan councils and the virgins of their voices in church affairs.

The Jesuits found it easier to deal with the clan councils than with the virgins. The councils chiefly managed church property and scheduled missioners' visits. As Europeran power spread into the interior of China, the Jesuits were able to move somewhat more openly into the hinterland and lay claim to church property under an imperial proclamation of March 18, 1846, which restored the missionaries' old lands to them. As the Jesuits took over the properties, the role of the clan councils melted away.

The virgins were harder to subdue, their role not being so dependent on external factors like land ownership. Their status was extraordinary. In conventional Chinese society, single women who were not widows carried a social and moral stigma. Yet in the eyes of fellow Christians, the virgins' important religious role justified their deviation from convention. The Jesuits set out to discredit the virgins and deny them a role in church affairs. Where they could—the virgins' resistance was prolonged—the foreign priests refused the virgins their customary leadership at worship services and sought to silence them altogether. To shadow their moral standing, the Jesuits announced that the only way of Christian perfection was a cloistered life lived in accordance with canon law and vows of poverty, chastity, and obedience. The missionary priests announced that cloistered French Sisters would train single Chinese women, the virgins especially, in that "perfect" way of life. Their religious role torn from them and their way of life branded as imperfectly Christian, the virgins were exposed to moral obloquy and discredited in their own communities.

The Jesuits might not have succeeded in their efforts against the clan councils and the virgins had not the Christian communities been devastated during the Taiping Rebellion of 1850-64. More correctly a revolution than a rebellion, the Taiping movement was an attempt by Hakka and Han Chinese to overthrow the Confucian order of the Manchus and to substitute an egalitarian social order. Evangelical Christianity was an important ingredient in the Taiping ideology. Despite a few initial instances in which the iconoclastic Taipings destroyed Catholic images of Mary and the saints because they thought them to be Buddhist images, the Taipings were generally friendly to their Catholic brethren. A contemporary report by a Protestant observer late in the war, however, claims Taipings persecuted some Catholics. Subsequently, Jesuit historians claimed that the Taipings destroyed almost all the Catholic villages and persecuted isolated Catholics; as a result, the Catholics fled to Shanghai seeking Jesuit assistance.[6]

It is possible that the Taipings did turn against the Catholics. Frustrated by setbacks, the Taipings knew that the Jesuits were acting as quartermasters and interpreters for the European powers. Friendly Taiping overtures were spurned and the Manchu enemy strengthened. The revolutionaries may then have drawn the erroneous conclusion that the Chinese Catholics were allies of the Jesuits. It is equally possible that the Jesuits, long friends of the Manchu dynasty and compulsively anti-egalitarian, were blind to the savage dynamics of a Manchu counteroffensive designed to purge all non-Confucian elements from Chinese society.

Whether by design of one side or the senselessness of war, Chinese Catholic villages were destroyed. Once dependent upon the French priests to whom they had fled, the Catholics could not resist the missioners' claims. With the restoration of order, the churches were rebuilt with European money and the increasingly numerous Jesuits were able to maintain a presence in more areas of their vicariate. As the Jesuit historian Colombel wrote: "From that time even in the temporal order the priest was under no obligation to the Christians, but on the contrary the Christians received almost everything from the priests. The relations of the priest to his Christians were no longer what they had been before the rebellion. The priest was really master in his church, leader of his Christianity [community of Christians]."[7]

By destroying the Chinese form of church organization, the Jesuits in Jiangnan made certain that the Catholic Church in China would be patterned upon the Roman model, which featured the dominance of a numerous clergy and the subordination of the laity, even though, as Colombel noted, lay Catholic leaders were often more intelligent and able than the missionary clergy.[8] It required women to accept life in cloister, with its economic dependency and legal subordination, as the price for even marginal status in the ecclesiastical structure. There was no room in it for the powerful role played by the virgins and as a result the Church tended to lose contact with Chinese women and to become an exclusively male organization, a fundamental defect.

Despite the imposition of the Roman church model, Chinese Catholics, both clergy and laity, managed to impart a distinct measure of communal church government to parish life when Chinese priests eventually controlled individual mission stations. An American Catholic missionary remarked of the situation in South China during the twentieth century:

> By training and character [the Chinese priest] is less venturesome off the beaten path and, outside routine, is more apt to leave direction to the Christians as a body.
>
> This tendency towards group action, characteristic of the Chinese

in general, has its advantages in church work as it unites the scattered Christian families and gives them an influence beyond their numerical strength, but it demands greater strength in their leader to effect his will. In church management it has the defects of the old trustee system in America and the good qualities of modern Catholic Action.

Its visible effect in mission work under a Chinese pastor is an increase of cooperation, especially in financial ways, and consequently a slowing down in the tempo of parish activities, due to more limited means; there is more uniformity and less individuality in the parish work. . . .[9]

Despite the failure of the Jesuits to eradicate the Chinese cultural tendency toward group action, the Counterreformation in China achieved its basic goals. And while the Jesuits stood out in their determination to reform the Church in China for their own benefit, they were not alone in their pursuit of a privileged position in the Catholic Church. For example, the Vincentians, who had worked in Sichuan, Macao, Hebei, Henan, Zhejiang, and Jiangxi, forced a second-class status upon the Chinese priests in their ecclesiastical jurisdictions. Even those Chinese secular priests whom they trained and permitted to enter their missionary congregation suffered an inferior position. This status was questioned at the 1851 Ningbo General Assembly of Vincentian China mission superiors. The General Assembly declared that European Vincentians should treat Chinese Vincentians "everywhere and in all things as confreres and even, if by their piety and obedience the Chinese make themselves worthy, to confer upon them jobs for which they are judged capable." The assembled Vincentian superiors immediately followed that statement with another qualification: "Nonetheless, it is necessary for many reasons to see to it that the Chinese confreres do not forget that it is to them after God, that the Chinese are indebted for their education and all the other advantages which they enjoy.[10]

The Growth of the Missionary Movement and Chinese Resistance

Foreign dominance within the Catholic Church reflected and was based upon the foreigners' privileged status in China, a status formulated in treaties and in less formal arrangements forced upon China by the West and Japan. Without their treaty privileges, the missionaries probably would not have been able to expand and consolidate their position after the Second Opium War.

Missionaries, Protestants and especially Catholics, began to move in ever greater numbers into the hinterland after the Second Opium War. French consular officials showed great concern for the priests and used their presence as an excuse to interfere in Chinese affairs. But the French officials and those of other nations appreciated that the missionaries were more than mere stalking horses. The missionaries' benevolent religious activities provided all foreigners with a certain assurance of the morality of their conduct and a cultural connection with distant homelands. Their medical, charitable and educational services were available to the foreigners and made life in China somewhat less hazardous and harsh. They counterbalanced to a degree the fundamentally exploitative nature of the foreign presence and created a large clientele which was not totally at the mercy of Chinese officials and land-owners. This clientele posed a threat to the local power structure which the Chinese resented. From time to time Chinese resentment manifested itself in acts of violence against church property, Chinese Christians, missionaries, or foreign officials. (The most serious resistance, the Boxer Rebellion, occurred in 1900.) Foreign governments then exacted money from the Chinese as reparations and paid it to the missionary societies involved, which in turn used the money to add to their large and often lucrative investments, whose profits provided for still more missionary endeavors.[11] What the Chinese reparations did not provide, European and American Catholic contributions did.

As more European missionary groups became involved, the main ecclesiastical territories were split among them. There was a proliferation of ecclesiastical divisions and subdivisions (in descending rank: vicariates apostolic; prefectures apostolic; independent missions; missions). Among the missionary groups, however, there was little cooperation. Jesuits and Vincentians nourished their historic rivalry. Germans looked down upon Latins and especially upon the Spanish, while the French made no attempt to hide their disdain for non-Frenchmen, occidental or oriental. Whatever the factionalism, however, all shared certain problems: how to finance missionary work; how to reach the Chinese; how to indoctrinate potential converts; how to maintain the active allegiance of Chinese Catholics.

Catholic Missionary Activities

Although in the late nineteenth century some missionaries believed that Western traders would foster a taste among the Chinese for Western civilization, including Christianity,[12] the missionaries as a whole did not leave the growth of the Church to chance or natural increase. They proselytized vigorously, sometimes hastily. Backed by their homelands, the missionaries fostered this growth by intervening in lawsuits on behalf of converts and by maintaining many orphanages, dispensaries, schools, and some hospitals. They employed Chinese lay people called catechists who publicized the Catholic faith and instructed both potential converts and professed Catholics from the catechism, a book of church precepts arranged in question and answer format.

Certain missionary tactics were especially irksome to the Chinese. Priestly meddling in legal cases on behalf of actual or prospective Christians was so bitterly resented that in 1908 the Vatican ordered a halt to the practice. Thereafter, most Catholic missioners refrained from such activity, although there were exceptions. About 1910, a French Vincentian tried to achieve his goal of 20,000 converts in Xinfeng, Jiangxi province, by systematically intervening in litigation on behalf of his clients. Those with lawsuits pending embraced Christianity to win a favorable settlement. The one-eyed French priest spoke no Chinese but he successfully used shock tactics. When a case involving one of his flock was to be adjudicated, the missioner would go to the official's office, gesture violently at the magistrate, and, having worked himself up to a fever pitch, pluck out his glass eyeball and throw it on the table in front of the magistrate to make his point. The terrified official would then give the priest's client what he wanted. At least some of the failures later experienced in Xinfeng by other missionaries seem to have been due to the hard feelings aroused by this one-eyed Frenchman.[13]

Another source of friction between the Catholic missionaries and the Chinese was the orphanages for foundling girls operated by the Church. Those institutions, a major factor in the European development of the Church in China and one way of offsetting its failure to reach adult Chinese women, often were the butt of anti-Christian agitation. Because Catholic doctrine maintained that the sacrament of Baptism was necessary to ensure entrance into eternal bliss for dying youngsters, the missionaries wished to baptize as many moribund infants as possible. So they took sick as well as healthy youngsters into their orphanages. Large numbers of children thus came to die within the orphanage walls and non-Christian Chinese were often ready to believe the worst of the missionaries.

Even had all the infants survived, the orphanages would have caused difficulties for the Church. William Hinton in his classic work, *Fanshen*, described the operation of a Dutch Franciscan-controlled orphanage in Long Bow village, Lucheng county, Shanxi province. Having noted that even very young orphans produced goods which were sold at a profit by the orphanage, Hinton observed that the older girls, who worked as long as twelve to fourteen hours a day in the orphanage, were betrothed in their early teens to local men for a "substantial remuneration." Athough this bride price was about a third lower than the average in the region, the Church was the main source of unpromised brides and it required prospective bridegrooms to become Catholics and to raise their children as such. As a result, "many poor peasants who wanted to get married had little alternative but to buy a Catholic wife."[14]

The orphanages and the advertising campaigns that accompanied them in the United States and Europe furnished Protestant missionaries with propaganda to use against the Roman Catholics. Thus although the American Dominicans had only one very small orphanage attached to their Fujian province mission, Protestant missionaries in Fuzhou, the provincial capital, told the Chinese that American Catholics were broadcasting the charge that Chinese were cruel to their children. Naturally, the Chinese resented such publicity and the Dominicans in China warned their confreres in America to put an end to it.[15]

Schools, too, played a significant role in Catholic efforts to reach the Chinese. Country mission schools, where children learned rudimentary reading skills, were widespread and there was an extensive network of primary schools conducted both by foreign and Chinese clergy and by the laity. In a country where literacy was the exception, these rudimentary schools made a valuable contribution to Chinese society. Furthermore, the Catholic clergy pioneered in developing a printed literature in conversational style for the ordinary Chinese. It would be decades before Chinese secular society would abandon the inaccessible epigrammatic classical language in its determination to break with the old order.[16] Only then did ordinary non-Christian Chinese gain access to written Chinese.

In secondary and higher education the Catholic Church did little, however, and its influence in learned circles was small. By 1914, Vatican authorities and a few missionaries in China were deeply troubled by the great influence of Protestant schools and colleges, where the medium of instruction was the popular English language.

The Chinese Catholic demand for English-medium instruction had begun well before the start of the twentieth century. As early as 1891, a Jesuit scholastic (a Jesuit in training for the priesthood) of the Missouri province, William Hornsby, taught English in the Portugese Jesuit school in Macao. Hornsby remained in China for twelve years, until ill health forced him to return to the United States. In that period he became the first American-born person to be ordained a priest in China and accompanied Dewey's fleet to the battle of Manila Bay.[17] A number of scholastics from the Jesuits' Southern U.S.A. (New Orleans) province taught English in the French Jesuit school in Tianjin. At the time when English was the commercial language of China's ports, these scattered Americans were able to supply the English-medium instruction desperately needed in European Jesuit schools. Their work, however, by no means filled the growing need, particularly in Beijing and Shanghai. The French Jesuits, for their part, conducted French-medium instruction at Aurora University in Shanghai.

Some Chinese Catholics were troubled that less than one percent of their fellow Catholics were literate and that the ill-educated Chinese clergy lacked influence with the Chinese intelligentsia. One of the concerned laity, Ying Lianzhi, took steps that led to the foundation of Fu Ren University, the Catholic University of Beijing. But even the bright promise of Fu Ren could not offset the intellectual failure of the Church in higher education. This continuing failure so disturbed Roman authorities that in the mid-1930s the former apostolic delegate to China, Celso Costantini, proposed abandoning pastoral work in the countryside and turning to secondary and higher education in China.[18]

Catholic religious instruction was not evangelical but catechetical. The missionary and his catechists did not preach the Gospel; they taught the catechism. Details of the procedure varied from region to region. In general, those Chinese who wished for one reason or another to be associated with the Roman Catholic Church came to live at the mission compound for three to twelve weeks or longer. While there, they memorized the catechism with the aid of the priest and catechists. During this period, known as the catechumenate—a name also given to the structure built to lodge the doctrine students—the missionary usually supported the students, who were known as catechumens. In the catechumenate period, the would-be Catholics also learned simple prayers and attended Mass and other religious ceremonies. If the catechumen persevered and learned the catechism, he or she might ask for baptism.

There were drawbacks to the catechumenate system. Some non-Christians attended merely to obtain free room and board and relief from the monotony of village life. The priests, sisters, and catechists were not always effective teachers and sometimes swelled conversion statistics by baptizing persons with little understanding of their new commitment. Even where understanding and commitment were the highest sort, the individual was usually returning to a non-Christian, sometimes anti-Christian environment; a new-found faith often withered for lack of reinforcement. Some missionaries, Americans included, thought that the isolation of Catholics was the chief obstacle to the spread of Catholicism. Consequently, many missionaries refused to baptize adults whose spouses did not convert to Christianity.

Catholic missionaries pursued a strategy of hasty doctrinal instruction and baptism well into the twentieth century. The results, on paper, were impressive. Despite the murder of thousands of Catholics during the Boxer Rebellion of 1900, the number of Catholics climbed from the First Opium War level of under 200,000 to 742,000 by the turn of the century and to 1,000,000 in 1907. Nominal membership passed 2,000,000 in 1921 and, at a greatly reduced rate of growth, reached, churchmen claimed, 3,000,000 in 1937. Careful examination of the 1936 ecclesiastical statistics, however, reveals that a third of the adults carried on the rolls did not practice their religion.[19]

Problems Facing the Catholic Church in China

Although the growth of the Catholic Church in China continued, many factors led to a slowdown in the rate of growth. Foremost among these were the collapse of stable government and the rise of Chinese nationalism. To quash mid-nineteenth-century rebels and fight foreign powers with designs on Indochina and Korea, the Manchus developed regional armies under strong military leaders. These regional forces became stronger than the central government. When the Manchus attempted to rebuild their relative power by mortgaging China's resources to foreigners, the Chinese revolted in 1911 and formed a republic the following year.

The Chinese republican government never effectively controlled all of China. Even at its strongest, under Jiang Jieshi (Chiang Kai-shek), it was a shifting coalition of regional and provincial warlords and politicians who fought among themselves and squeezed the peasantry to pay for their deadly struggles. Little distinguished the government military units from the bandit gangs which plagued the countryside. Under these circumstances, missionaries found it hard to reach Chinese Christians and to keep Christian communities intact. The priests made it a policy, however, to open their mission churches and compounds to Christians and non-Christians alike whenever danger threatened.

These were also the years of rising Chinese nationalism and growing antiforeign sentiment, double forces which embarrassed the Catholic Church, which was still identified with foreign powers. Many Chinese hesitated to join the Church on those grounds alone. To complicate matters, some missioners, Americans included, were publicly unsympathetic to Chinese nationalism. Communist antiforeign and antireligious activities also hurt the operation of the Church in some areas, as did floods and famines. Finally, harassment by the Japanese in Manchuria from 1932 and later in other areas of China hampered the Catholic Church.

Internal problems began to be felt by the end of World War I. The failure to develop English-language secondary schools and colleges has already been mentioned. World War I reduced the ranks of the clergy catastrophically, as French, Belgians, and Germans responded to draft calls and went to serve in their nations' armed forces. Since the French constituted the majority of the Catholic foreign missioners, the recall of healthy Frenchmen of military age left French missions unmanned in some areas, notably in Guangdong, Guangxi, and Manchuria.

Following the war, Chinese authorities repatriated from Shandong and Fujian provinces at least eighteen German missionaries, those not "necessary to the continuity of the work." In Fujian and Hunan provinces, active Spanish missioners were few. In all these areas, proselytization had slowed or stopped altogether; what remained was often superficial.

The prospects for the Church in Central China were not particularly bright in those early postwar years. Not only were the Italian Franciscans who worked in the Wuhan (Hankow) area unable to provide English-medium instruction, but they were unable to operate an effective urban ministry. One American friar who had worked with the Italians for some years was unsympathetic to their desire to hold on to the cities of Wuhan and Wuchang. He urged the Belgian friar who headed the Franciscans' mission bureau in Rome to adopt the "radical remedy" of "putting such people in the backwoods where they belong and put[ting] some Franciscans [i.e., American Franciscans] in Wuchang who will give us more hopes of success."[20]

Incoming American missionaries, drafted by the Vatican to fill the depleted ranks in China, would soon learn at first hand the inflated membership claims and institutional weaknesses of the Roman Church in China.

2

Sources and Dynamics of the American Catholic China Missions

The Vatican's Concern for the China Missions

By 1915, officials of the Vatican's mission secretariat, Propaganda Fide, were clearly worried about the missions in China. Protestant influence was growing among the urban Chinese and some Chinese Catholics were insisting that Rome send to China English-speaking foreign missionaries. The sources of English-speaking clergy and religious would have to be Ireland and the United States. But because they lived among Protestants, American Catholics were a suspect group in European Catholic eyes. Furthermore, religious societies based in the United States were generally reluctant to undertake mission work. If the Vatican could recruit Irish and American missionaries, it would still have to deal with the government of France, which claimed to be the secular protector of the China missions and used them as an excuse for political activity in China. The French authorities might balk at the presence of Irish and American Catholics. The European mission societies themselves would certainly be reluctant to cede their territories to church workers of other societies, especially those of other nations. Finally, and not least of all, nationalism was beginning to emerge among the Chinese clergy.

The Protestant challenge to Catholicism in China was enormous. Some Protestant commentators labeled their activities the "Christian occupation of China." A widespread network of organizations had built up zeal for the China missions to crusading pitch by the early years of the twentieth century, a time of epic Jewish and Catholic immigration into the United States.[1] As American Protestants fretted that their way of life was being endangered, they increased their contributions to foreign missions. Almost $19,000,000 was contributed in 1915, double the amount given in 1904. Mission property in China was estimated to be worth at least $30,000,000. By 1926, there would be 8235 American Protestants in the China missions deeply involved in spreading Protestant influence through direct evangelization and educational, medical, and social work. Their English-medium educational work was especially influential.

In addition to European reluctance to cede territory, other obstacles hampered any Vatican program to counter Protestant influence in China. The uncertain supply of English-speaking Catholic missionaries from the United States and Ireland was a major impediment. As a far smaller and much poorer country, Ireland did not have the potential the United States had for providing and supporting missionaries. Many Roman Catholic communities in the United States, however, were riven with dissension and seemed to Rome to be tainted with Protestantism.

The Distress of Roman Catholicism in the United States

Well into the twentieth century Roman Catholicism in the United States had unsettled political and cultural identities. At the turn of the century, Catholic clergymen found it necessary to fight a lengthy battle for control against laymen arriving from Eastern Europe with the expectation of controlling the parishes in which they lived.[2] The Catholic Church was also the scene of a bitter debate over Catholicism's relation to American culture and society. Almost to the end of the nineteenth century, the Irish-dominated secular (diocesan) clergymen thought that they had triumphed over the European-oriented religious orders, champions of the preservation of old ways, and had established once and for all a Catholic pattern of accommodation to American society. Then they suffered a stunning setback. In 1899 Pope Leo XIII condemned a nebulous heresy called "Americanism" (which, among other things, allegedly called into question the claim of the religious orders to being the perfect way of Christian life). Leo did not directly accuse the accommodationists of being "Americanists" but his action weakened their cause and threw them on the defensive. Another blow followed in 1907 when Leo's successor, Pius X, attacked the heresy of "modernism."

These developments increased the tensions within American Catholicism and made it increasingly conservative. Ecclesiastical witch-hunting spread through Europe and America; seminary training took on the most rigid of doctrinaire European approaches and original thought disappeared from American Catholic theological circles.[3] German-American Catholicism, the bulwark of nonaccommodationism, enjoyed a new lease on life. Its champions maintained their bitter campaign against the policies of the Irish-American church leaders.[4] The German-Americans claimed that the English-speaking clergy had betrayed the church by casting off European Catholic culture thereby loosening the bonds between the church and many Catholics. The accommodationists denied the charge.[5]

Satisfied that the accommodationists had been sufficiently chastised, Rome did not want to alienate the leadership or the laity of the world's most vigorous and wealthy body of Roman Catholics. So in 1908 it soothed the chastened American Catholic church leaders by removing them from the supervision of Propaganda Fide. Officially, the Roman Catholic Church in America had come of age; it was no longer a mission church.

The Vatican's administrative gesture of approval was so ambiguous that it made little real difference to the Catholic Church in the United States. Both the accommodationists and their foes were able to claim that it signaled approval of their policies. Certainly it did not remove the cloud over the accommodationists and their policies nor did it deliver Catholics from the nativist, anti-Catholic pressures which characterized American society.

Developments in the United States seemingly justified the Vatican's confidence in its disciplinary measures. Handsome dividends accrued to the papacy as a result of its diplomatic finesse in dealing with the Americans. Church rolls expanded until there were more than 16,000,000 nominal Catholics in the United States in 1916, one-third of the nation's church members. The number of priests was also growing.[6]

Foreign Missionary Activity as a Response to Distress

Many American Catholics suffered the double bind of being neither Roman Catholic enough for Rome nor American enough for American Protestants because of their Catholicism. The resulting tension produced the Catholic Foreign Mission Society of America, known more commonly as the Maryknoll Society, after Maryknoll, the hilltop site of its seminary near Ossining, New York. Founded in 1911, Maryknoll was the brainchild of two American diocesan priests, Thomas F. Price and James A. Walsh. Price, a failure as a home missionary in North Carolina, was the living embodiment of the Catholic Church's failure to convert American Protestantism and its subsequent turning away to foreign mission work. Walsh, a proponent of the notion that the American Catholic community had to prove itself apostolically sound (thoroughly and actively Roman) by undertaking foreign mission work, embodied American Catholics' distress that the Vatican did not accept them as true Roman Catholics. Each priest thus personified half of American Catholicism's dilemma and it is not strange that they came together to relieve their social and religious anxiety.

The methods used to cultivate support for the China missions revealed a sensitivity to the frustrations plaguing American Catholics. Mission publicists sought to gather alms and recruit volunteers by portraying China as a vast and important battleground where Catholics fought wealthy American Protestants. Thus the editor of *Catholic Missions* wrote in March 1914:

> China is the largest mission field of the world and great efforts are centered upon it to Christianize it. Catholicism and Protestantism are

vying in zeal to uproot paganism from that promising land. The means placed at the disposal of our Catholic missionaries are much less than the resources of the Protestant missionaries. The ratio in favor of the Protestants [16+:1] is probably even superior to the ratio of contributions mentioned in the forepart of this article.[7]

The editor's anxiety over greater Protestant resources surfaced again the following year but by 1918 he was complaining that mission benefactors were all stipulating that their donations go to the China missions.[8] In light of this trend the Jesuit editors of *America* felt confident that Catholic missionaries in China would be able to employ their substantial but smaller resources more effectively than their Protestant competitors.[9]

Although the American laity was pouring significant sums into the missions and particularly the China missions,[10] no institution could guarantee potential missionaries work in China. Only the newly formed Catholic Foreign Mission Society of America held out the possibility of concentration upon China mission work and when it finally opened a mission in China it quickly captured the allegiance of most would-be Catholic missionaries. With its parallel organization for women, the society became the foremost symbol of the missionary spirit among American Catholics.

The Entry of American Catholics into the China Missions

The Vatican could not use the small group of men training with the Maryknoll Society to redress the immediate shortage of Catholic missionaries in China. The shortage intensified at the end of World War I when the Chinese government repatriated at least eighteen German missionaries from Shandong and Fujian provinces.[11] The situation would have been worse had not the Vatican caused the American hierarchy to persuade the State Department to have the Chinese government leave some Germans in the missions.[12] The Vatican also put increasing pressure on mission societies either to send China more priests, especially English-speaking priests, or to give up their missions. In light of the French government's interests in the continuation of the French missions, most of the Vatican's pressure was on Italian and Spanish mission societies. These societies proved to be parochial, defensively nationalistic, and reluctant to welcome Irish or American Catholic missionary organizations.

The experience of the Maryknoll co-founder, James A. Walsh, while seeking a place in East Asia for the members of his new Catholic Foreign Mission Society of America illustrated one aspect of the Vatican's problem. Walsh's institution was initially conceived only as an analog to the Paris Foreign Mission, i.e., as a seminary which would offer to foreign bishops and vicars apostolic the services of the priests whom it trained. Until he finally found a bishop, Monsignor de Guebriant, Vicar Apostolic of Guangzhou, willing to have Maryknollers work in his territory, Walsh had been unable to persuade any of the European mission leaders in China to accept the services of his men. Walsh's long and frustrating pilgrimage to East Asia had nearly ended in a failure which probably would have meant the end of his organization. Without China mission work, Maryknoll would not have attracted recruits.

United States consular officials in China gave the Catholic Foreign Mission Society of America a warmer welcome. James A. Walsh later recalled, "When I talked with the Consul at Shanghai on the occasion of my first visit to China, he expressed his delight at the advent of American priests, believing it would add to the prestige of the American Government. I told him quite plainly that we were not coming for that purpose, although we loved our country and would be pleased if our presence reacted favorably in any way on our country. He saw the point of view but remarked on the tremendous value [of] the French missionary influence as affecting France."[13]

Because missionaries were so closely tied to questions of political prestige, the Vatican wished to avoid a direct confrontation with the French government over the issue of replacing French missionaries with American counterparts in a province so close to French Indochina. It was therefore content to allow de Guebriant and other French ecclesiastics to negotiate directly with American mission groups. The French ecclesiastics were sensitive to the political issues involved. De Guebriant, for example, was careful to assure himself of his government's acquiescence in the expanding Maryknoll presence in Guangdong province. Moreover, both he and the Maryknollers strove successfully to maintain cordial mutual relations. One reason for this accomplishment was the willingness of the Americans to reimburse the French for the property turned over to the Maryknollers. With these monies and some Maryknoll alms, the displaced French clergy, who depended on mission work for their livelihood, were able to establish new missions in the territories remaining to them.

In Jiangxi, French Lazarists were unwilling to admit American confreres into the Yujiang and Ganzhou territories. Perhaps because Jiangxi was farther away from politically sensitive Indochina and Zhanjiang (Ft. Bayard), Guangdong, the Vatican exerted strong pressure on the Congregation of the Mission to send American members or give up the missions.[14] At length the Congregation, which, like the Maryknoll group, needed missions to survive, gave in and sent American confreres to work under the French. In 1921, the Eastern U.S.A. province sent nine men to Ganzhou. In August 1922, the Congregation's Western U.S.A. province received orders to send men to Yujiang, one of the richest missions in China.

The Vatican was generally more forceful in dealing with non-French groups. In 1920, the American branch of the Congregation of the Most Sacred Cross and Passion of Our Lord Jesus Christ, better known as the

PROVINCES of CHINA

0   300 kilometers

0   300 statute miles

SOURCES: United States Central Intelligence Agency, China, May 1979.
Urban missions from J.B. Prud'homme, S.J., Missions Catholiques en Chine, 2nd ed., 1936.

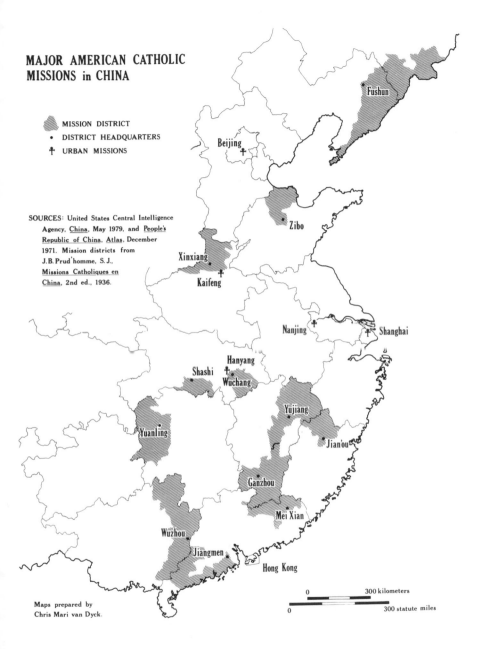

MAJOR AMERICAN CATHOLIC MISSIONS in CHINA

- ▨ MISSION DISTRICT
- • DISTRICT HEADQUARTERS
- † URBAN MISSIONS

SOURCES: United States Central Intelligence
Agency, China, May 1979, and People's
Republic of China, Atlas, December
1971. Mission districts from
J.B. Prud'homme, S. J.,
Missions Catholiques en
China, 2nd ed., 1936.

Fushun

Beijing †

Zibo

Xinxiang
†
Kaifeng

Nanjing †

Shanghai †

Hanyang
Shashi †
Wuchang

Yujiang

Yuanling

Jian'ou

Ganzhou

Mei Xian

Wuzhou

Jiangmen

Hong Kong

0   300 kilometers

0   300 statute miles

Maps prepared by
Chris Mari van Dyck.

Passionists, obeyed an order of the congregation's highest body to expand as quickly as possible especially into non-Christian lands, and offered its services to the Vatican for mission work in China. Propaganda Fide countered with an offer of a mission in Xizang (Tibet) since, it reasoned, a branch of this rather monastic group would be attractive in the citadel of Buddhist monasticism. Dismayed, the American Passionists complained that they could not handle such a mission. Propaganda Fide then told the Augustinian Order to hand over its Yuanling mission in northwestern Hunan to the Passionists. The Augustinian leadership resisted until it learned from its American branch that for some years to come there would be no available American Augustinians.[15]

The Protestant threat moved the Vatican to dismember the Italian Franciscan missions in the central Chang Jiang (Yangtze) Valley around Hanyang, Wuchang, and Wuhan. To mollify the Friars Minor, it first offered an unpromising outlying portion of their Wuchang territory to the Irish Columban Fathers. The Irish refused it and demanded something more promising. The Vatican then gave the Irish the Hanyang mission on the other side of the Chang Jiang. Rather than yield more territory, the Friars Minor leadership in Rome ordered its four American provinces (New York, Cincinnati, St. Louis, and San Francisco) to undertake a joint mission effort in Wuchang.[16]

The American Franciscans were well aware of the Vatican's motives in recruiting them for China. The leader of the Friars Minor clearly laid out the anti-Protestant nature of the mission when he told the Americans that the purpose of the mission was to "offset the most nefarious propagandism practised by the Englisch [sic] sectarians in China."[17]

Anti-Protestant crusading in a distant land had no great appeal for many American Friars Minor. Volunteers were slow to step forward and by late 1923 there were only six newly arrived friars in Wuchang. Nonetheless, Propaganda Fide quickly redivided the Vicariate of Eastern Hubèi and by decree of December 12, 1923, made the six-county area around Wuchang into a prefecture apostolic subject to the Americans. The Cincinnati province assumed responsibility for the mission as Rome ordered the Americans to take on still another territory in 1924. Care of nineteen counties of the German Franciscans' Jinan, Shandong, mission fell to the St. Louis, Missouri, province.[18]

Vatican insistence was also responsible for the American Dominicans' mission in Jian'ou, Fujian. About 1918 Rome began to exert pressure on the American Dominican Province of St. Joseph to undertake mission work. The head of the province, Raymond Meagher, O.P., was reluctant to divert his province's resources to China. He resisted until 1922, when he inspected the 3000-square-mile area around Jian'ou, Fujian, which Rome wished to assign to his province. Thirty years of work by Spanish and Filipino friars of the

Spanish-Filipino Province of the Holy Rosary had produced only 700 Catholics and 2000 catechumens from a population of 1,000,000.[19] After viewing the bleak prospects in Fujian and reviewing the needs of his expansionary program in the United States, Meagher took ten minutes from his schedule to tell Rev. Paul Curran that Curran and Brother Alfred Sullivan were going to China. Only on his way across the United States did Curran learn that he would be superior of the Jian'ou mission.[20]

The Vatican was also responsible for the presence of American Benedictines in China. Yielding to longstanding appeals from Chinese Catholics for English-speaking missionaries who could staff a university, the Vatican looked to the Benedictine Order to provide them. As early as 1912 an influential Catholic layman, Ying Lianzhi (Vincent Ying), who was a co-founder and editor-in-chief of the *Da Gong Bao*, a progressive Tianjin newspaper, had appealed to Pope Pius X to establish a Catholic university in Beijing. Ying continued to advocate the idea and in late 1920 spoke of it to a visiting seminary professor at the Benedictine Order's St. Vincent's Archabbey at Latrobe, Pa. The professor, Dr. George Barry O'Toole, raised the issue in Rome with Pope Benedict XV and with the Abbot Primate of the Benedictine Order, Dom Fidelis Stotzingen. Benedictine authorities followed the Vatican's lead in suggesting to the American Cassinese Congregation of the Benedictine Order that it begin a Catholic university in Beijing. Unwilling to refuse, the Congregation asked St. Vincent's Archabbey to undertake the task. The Archabbey complied and in a rescript dated June 27, 1924, Pope Pius XI conferred upon the Archabbot of St. Vincent's full power to appoint staff and to regulate the courses of the proposed university. The Archabbot in turn appointed George B. O'Toole as Rector.[21]

Another American mission which stemmed from the Vatican's receptivity to Chinese advocacy was the American Jesuit presence in Shanghai and Nanjing. Lu Pahang, a Shanghai magnate and leading Catholic layman, took the initiative in finding English-speaking Jesuits to begin educational work in his city. While attending the 1926 Eucharistic Congress in Chicago, he discussed the matter with the head of the Jesuits' California province. Lu then went to Rome and discussed his idea with Pope Pius XI and with the Father General of the Society of Jesus, Wlodimir Ledochowski. Both approved of the project but Ledochowski stipulated that Lu obtain the consent of the vicar apostolic of Shanghai, Prosper Paris, S.J., and Lu did so.[22]

The Vatican's reliance on formal ecclesiastical groups for American Catholic clergy was virtually complete because it could not tap the pool of diocesan clergy. These were ordained for work in one diocese and might work elsewhere only of their own volition and with the consent of their bishop and the bishop of the place to which they wished to transfer. Some joined the Maryknoll group or other religious societies and thus made themselves available for mission work. Only by exception did diocesan priests transfer directly into a mission diocese. Two who did so were Fr. Howard P. Lawton of the Philadelphia archdiocese and Francis Clougherty of the Pittsburgh diocese. They were the only two secular priests whom Monsignor Noah Tacconi, the Italian leader of the Kaifeng, Henan, mission was able to recruit during an extensive tour of the United States in 1919. In this instance the pronounced anti-Italian feeling among the American Catholic clergy may have reinforced the normal reluctance of the diocesan clergy to transfer into mission work.[23]

Because it could not compel diocesan clergy, members of religious sister-hoods, or laypersons to go to China, the Vatican had to rely for missionary personnel on the continuing cooperation of the male groups already described and on the voluntary collaboration of several religious sisterhoods. These groups made balky collaborators, each with its own interests and problems.

Problems in Staffing the Missions

The maintenance of an adequate missionary force in China was a difficult task which faced all of the groups. Initial enthusiasm for China mission work was often short-lived. In 1925, for example, only four years after the departure of the first Passionists band for China, Passionist authorities had trouble finding volunteers for that mission. In 1924, only three years after they began work in Ganzhou, Jiangxi, American Vincentians were disturbed to hear that confreres were refusing to go to China. In 1928, the provincial superior of the Vincentians' Western U.S.A. province polled nearly twenty of his priests and found only three who would go willingly. Two of the three were over forty, the third almost as old and, in the provincial superior's mind, unsuited. The provincial superior referred the matter to the Vincen-tian superior general, asking him either to relieve his province of the Yujiang vicariate or to suggest ways to obtain recruits.[24]

The provincial superiors were not eager to send personnel, especially the more highly talented, to China. They wished instead to expand and improve their domestic programs. Thus the leadership of the Vincentians' Western U.S.A. province preferred to open and staff seminaries in Denver, Los Angeles, and Kansas City rather than send reinforcements to Yujiang. The provincial superiors of the Jesuits' California province decided that only a handful of their more talented young men could be spared for work in China and proceeded to make their China mission into a repository for the less talented. Even the Maryknoll group began to divert its more promising men away from at least one of its South China missions as it expanded across the United States and into other foreign lands.[25]

In response to irresistible pressure from Rome, some organizations took strong measures to increase the number of their missionaries in China. The Dominican provincial superior ruthlessly used China as a dumping ground for misfits and disturbed personnel. He sent at least one man to Jian'ou as a penance. When few of their subordinates volunteered for China, superiors of the Jesuits' California province sent men against their will. Perhaps as many as half of the American Jesuits who went to China from the California province went involuntarily. The Vincentians sent some of their troublesome members to China. That congregation, according to its Vicar Apostolic of Yujiang, sent out some men with "funny ways" and alcoholic tendencies, as well as at least one man who didn't try to learn the language or accommodate himself to China. Thus four of the fifteen American missionaries in the Yujiang vicariate apostolic were more or less ineffective.[26]

The religious sisterhoods which joined in the China missions usually exhibited a higher degree of initial enthusiasm for missionary work than did the male groups but their enthusiasm was no more durable. Nor was the leadership of the sisterhoods reluctant to fill mission bands with superannuated, disturbed, or disturbing personnel. As a result, some groups such as the Dominican Sisters in Fujian quickly lost key personnel to death, while others such as the Maryknoll Sisters in Hong Kong and the Franciscan Sisters in Wuchang suffered badly from poor leadership. Nonetheless, the sisterhoods in general were to render valuable service to the Church and to the Chinese.

European Resentment and Chinese Resistance

When these groups reached China they did not usually find a cordial reception from their forerunners. In Guangdong and Guangxi, the warm reception given to the Maryknoll missionaries by the priests of the Paris Foreign Mission was a marked exception to the general pattern. In Yujiang, for example, American Vincentians received a cold welcome from their ardent Francophile confrere, Monsignor Clerc-Renaud, and in Shandong German Franciscans allowed the mission territory about to be turned over to the Americans to deteriorate. This pattern of grudging cession and scarcely veiled resentment toward the Americans was common.

The ordinary missionary pattern was for an American society to dispatch priests to work under the supervision of a European bishop until they could manage themselves and the mission. But the Spanish Augustinians left the American Passionists on their own so quickly and so abruptly that the new missionaries were convinced that the Europeans were intent on sabotaging them.[27] The Spanish-Filipino Dominicans in Fujian were even less helpful to their American successors.

Failure to break free of initial European domination occurred only once in the case of American Catholic male missionaries to China and the results, for the American Jesuits involved, were bitter. The French dominated the modern Jesuit missions in China. Their great establishment at Xujiawei

outside Shanghai was a monument to nineteenth-century European architecture, to the futility of seeking past grandeur in minute observance of
fossilized customs, and to the ease with which religious authority reinforced
French colonial ambitions. Forced to take on an undefined educational
mission in the Shanghai area, the California province of the Society of Jesus
sent a few priests and many younger men to work under the French Jesuits
there. Enormous energies were spent over many years in defining the
Americans' task. In the interim, the young men studied under French
authorities in the Jesuit seminary at Xujiawei, an institution known as "The
House of Ten Thousand Customs." French superiors kept an enervating
hold on the American and Chinese Jesuits subject to them. "Everything went
by numbers," one American Jesuit reminisced, "If you asked a superior
something, the first thing he'd do would be to pull out his epitome [rule book]
or custom book to find the answer."[28] At least two of the young American
Jesuits studying at Xujiawei suffered nervous breakdowns as a result of the
tight discipline. Those, such as Cornelius Lynch, who pointed out the
implications of French rule for the Church were sent home.

Ecclesiastical authority under canon law sometimes worked to the advantage of American missionaries. In Guangdong, for example, Maryknollers
were able to exclude Chinese priests from the Jiangmen territory. In Jiangxi,
the Vincentians of the Yujiang vicariate apostolic used canon law to quell an
attempt by Chinese clergy to control about half of the American territory. In
consultation during late 1934 with the Vatican's representative to China
(apostolic delegate), Archbishop Mario Zanin, the leader of the Americans,
Paul B. Misner, decided to break Chinese opposition by putting Americans
in charge of all the principal residences in the area held by the Chinese
priests. Misner and Zanin agreed that in the event of resistance by the
Chinese clergy "any malcontents are to be visited with the full vigor of the
Canon Law applied either by the Vicar Apostolic himself or directly by the
Delegation."[29]

Authority to enforce canon law had great economic significance for the
missionaries. It allowed the French to retain control over significant investments, as when Maryknollers sought unsuccessfully to obtain a portion of the
Boxer Indemnity Funds paid to the Shenyang (Mukden) vicariate apostolic.[30]
It permitted the Maryknollers to keep mission territory clear of Chinese
priests and thus open to further work by their society, which needed to
expand. It allowed the Vincentians not only to correct improper personal
conduct by some Chinese priests in the Yujiang vicariate apostolic but also to
ensure that the rapidly increasing and antiforeign Chinese clergy would not
gain control of "all the better places in the Vicariate." In that event, the
Americans would not have become leaders of well-appointed local churches
and would have lost their aura of superiority. As one Vincentian wrote of

these "better places," "If the Chinese should once get control under present conditions it would be impossible for a foreigner to work with them."[31]

The conflict in South China between the American and Chinese clergy underscores the contradiction between the needs of mission societies and individual missionaries on the one hand and the Roman Church's professed goal of developing an independent Chinese hierarchy and clergy on the other hand. Occidental pride compounded the economic reasons which spawned the pervasive missionary opposition to the growth of the Chinese clergy. When his superior told Fr. James F. Kearney, S.J., that he might be assistant to a Chinese pastor in a Shanghai Chinese parish (Gonzaga), he replied that "after preparing a year and a half to be pastor, and having mapped out a whole program it was very discouraging to end up as flunky to a young Chinese priest and I would prefer the Bush of Haichow to staying discontented at Gonzaga." Kearney did not become pastor, and as a result of his opposition neither did the Chinese priest.[32]

Female Catholic missionaries also clashed with Chinese churchwomen and generally entertained the same attitudes toward the Chinese as did their male counterparts. Chinese women who sought to enter foreign missionary societies or Chinese societies founded by the foreigners very often could not break free of the novice's lowly status after completing the required probationary period, the novitiate. Treated like servants by the Sisters, they resented their condition. A representative of the apostolic delegate to China remarked to the Sisters of Providence after inspecting their novitiate for a Chinese group, the Providence Sisters Catechists, which they had founded in 1929, "Oh, your Chinese Sisters all look so happy. They are not dissatisfied like so many other Chinese Sisters who are with foreign Sisters."[33] But some time thereafter some of the Providence Sisters Catechists turned against their foreign mentors.

Two American sisterhoods, the Maryknoll Sisters and the Sisters of Providence, established new Chinese sisterhoods and in each case the Americans tended to dominate the new groups. They brooked no opposition to their rule. When a Chinese novice Sister Catechist tried to stir up other novices and the older Sisters as well against the Sisters of Providence and to coordinate a mass petition asking that the foreign Sisters have nothing to do with their government, the American Sisters dismissed her and another plotter from the convent.[34] There is no record of subsequent resistance to their rule.

The Institutional Limitations of the Missionary Groups

In addition to the conflicts between foreigners of different nationalities and between foreigners and Chinese, there was also rivalry among the missionary groups. The root of this antagonism was the determination of each group to preserve its corporate identity and thus its claim to official ecclesiastical standing and to alms. Adherence to organizational forms and communal customs as well as close regulation of the lives of its members was believed to be the only way to ensure survival as a distinct group.

Emphasis on rule and authority especially marked the groups of missionary women. At the departure ceremony for the first band of Sisters of Loretto who left Nerinx, Kentucky, for Hanyang, Hubei province, in September 1923, each of the six new missionaries was handed a copy of the sisterhood's rulebook. When the Adorers of the Blood of Christ changed their rules, they sent a copy of the new rule book to their missionary Sisters in Bin Xian, Shandong province. A Sister noted in the mission annals the arrival of "the long-awaited Holy Rule. Deo Gratias! At last the treasure has arrived."[35]

Fear of the Chinese and of absorption into Chinese culture added to the ordinary institutional dynamic of self-preservation. Thus in 1924 Fr. Paul Ubinger, C.P., the superior of the Passionists in Hunan, wrote that each Passionist needed to live with at least one other Passionist so that they might recall their congregation's ideas and customs and thereby "counteract the evil influence of vain and deceitful Chinese ideas and customs." When American leaders of the Passionists decided that their China missionaries were drifting away from strict observance of Passionist rules and customs, observances which interfered with language study and which the Passionists knew the Chinese considered odd and unattractive, they sent a priest known for "Rigor, Narrowness, and Scrupulosity" to govern their group in China.[36]

Individual insecurity or instability sometimes strengthened the authoritarianism of the religious groups. The Maryknoll Sisterhood is a case in point. Originally an informal group of lay women assisting the Catholic Foreign Mission Society of America, it came under pressure from James A. Walsh to incorporate as a formal religious organization. Walsh desired to become the founder of an American sisterhood specifically oriented to foreign mission work. The group was also under similar pressure from some of its own members as well as prospective members who wished to achieve the definite role and status of "real Sisters." So the group adopted the rules and constitutions common to the sisterhoods of the Dominican Order. In the course of their training by a representative of the Dominican Sisters of Sinsinawa, Wisconsin, the lives of the women became filled with "unaccustomed formalities between subject and superior" and between one another as well. When their first band of missionaries reached Hong Kong on November 3, 1921, and settled into a small cottage in Kowloon, its Superior, Sister Mary McKenna, enforced an extremely strict religious discipline because she wanted to prove to skeptical local European Catholics that the sisterhood was truly Roman Catholic. In such an atmosphere the Sisters made little progress in learning the Chinese language.[37]

The Chinese congregations initiated by the Americans replicated the internal dynamics of Occidental groups. A Chinese Sister trained by the Maryknoll Sisters wrote that her life and the lives of her Sisters were governed by "canon law governing Congregations of Sisters with simple vows, vicariate rules governing mission work, a tentative directory, rules that are promulgated, altered or annulled as conditions prove necessary, and the [Jiangmen sisterhood's] constitutions; insofar as they agree with the life, work and aims of their particular congregation.[38]

Many observers in China recoiled at the sight of the missionaries' strange garb and customs and disciplinary practices. Ralph Townsend, former American consular official in Fuzhou, Fujian, wrote: "A fiercer burning piety, or at least a fiercer personal search for it, seems to animate the Catholic orders in China than is evident among the Protestants." He also commented: "The Catholics exert a discipline over their workers that strikes a bystander as needlessly cruel."[39]

The national and institutional bickering among missionary groups and the scandal felt by the Chinese because of church customs upset Vatican officials and they gave serious consideration to the abolition of the religious orders in China.[40] Yet they pulled back from such a step because it would have had serious repercussions among Catholics everywhere, including China. The abolition or suspension of corporate identities hallowed by time and generally protected by canon law might have caused many missionaries to defect and other personnel to refuse to go to China. The existing European missions might have collapsed altogether and the American and Irish Catholics might have refused to participate in the short-term strategy of introducing English-medium instruction into the Church's program.

One other canonically sanctioned condition which sorely embarrassed the Church's effectiveness in China but to which Vatican officials gave little or no attention was the canonical subordination of women to men and the enclaustration to one degree or another of women churchworkers. The failure of the Church to reach adult Chinese women was the most striking result of this policy. Indeed, the greater the presence of female church personnel, the closer the attention of church leaders, always men, to the enforcement of canon law. Thus, for example, in 1936 Monsignor Ambrose Pinger, O.F.M., prefect of the Zibo, Shandong, prefecture apostolic, wrote to the head of the Franciscan friars' St. Louis, Missouri, province requesting a canon lawyer because there were by that time three communities of Sisters in that mission.[41]

The success of the Vatican's short-term strategy for the China missions thus rested to a large degree on the ability of American Catholics to overcome difficulties posed by their own institutions, by other mission groups, and by the legal structure of the Church itself. In the process, American Catholic missionaries would also have to overcome the contradictions arising from their wealth and their association with the foreign powers. To these challenges were added the need to learn a new language and adjust to a different culture. The task was formidable and the circumstances unpromising.

3

Persons of Wealth and Power

Like the European clergy before them, the American Catholic missionaries to China readily assumed the role of agents of a rich and powerful institution. The Occident's wealth had generated power, which in turn protected its wealth. But the profligate waste of World War I seriously compromised the ability of the Western capitalist nations to project their power into the interior of China; capitalism could no longer protect its interests in China against the rising tide of antiforeignism. Among those interests was the Catholic Church with its personnel, wealth, and Chinese following.

Foreign tutors and Chinese assistants quickly taught the tyro American Catholic missionaries the routine of foreign mission work as well as the behavior that would be expected of them. With only a few exceptions the Americans were docile students and imitated the European priests and Sisters.

The Missionary Priests' Routine

Many American Catholics imagined that the lives of China missionaries were very difficult. F. X. Ford wrote his confreres, "Nothing but a consensus of statements from the thousands of missioners would actually bury the super-stition that life on the mission is superhuman . . . I have lived with country pastors and admired their perseverance in daily rounds of small matters in a narrow circle. That about sums up the life of the average missioner, as far as I can judge it." He succinctly explained the reason for the basic similarities: "If mission work was merely a matter of baptizing pagans we could not parallel it with home work, but actual evangelizing takes up but a small portion of the missioner's time."[1]

The mission pastor was the branch manager for one of the world's largest organizations. He was responsible for the day-to-day operation of an enterprise which provided a living for himself, foreign and native Sisters, catechists, teachers, seminarians, cooks, servants, and foundlings. It was his responsibility to enlarge the mission's clientele and to train a Chinese cadre.

The center of the missionary's life was the central mission station, usually a complex of church, rectory, schools, and garden, often enclosed with a high wall. Although the church architecture was generally European in style, each nationality seemed to leave its mark on the complex. A Chinese priest would grow vegetables where a foreigner would raise grass and flowers. From Guangdong, F. X. Ford commented on the differences in foreign tastes: "The French missioner leans towards perennials, especially rose bushes, and an attempt at a formal garden, though without undue attention to plan or primness; the Spaniard relies more on palm trees and a flagged courtyard; the German shows his nationality by whitewashed walls and spotless paths, while we Americans tend rather to variety and bright flowers and less picturesque but well repaired drains and wells."[2]

The complexes were imposing and occasionally overshadowed nearby villages. The Erbashi mission compound, which the Maryknollers of the Fushun, Manchuria, mission took over from the French, was surrounded by a gray brick wall ten feet high dominating the village. Inside the 200-by-300 foot compound was a dilapidated church attended by the village's 400 Catholics. The mission school held 100 students, many of whom boarded free at the mission.[3]

The missionary priest's routine of saying Mass, hearing confessions, supervising the work of catechists, Sisters, and schoolteachers, keeping accounts, administering simple remedies, reading the prayers of the breviary, and writing to stateside confreres and benefactors was broken up by periodic trips through the countryside to visit the mission outstations. These trips were especially arduous in the mountains of South China, but they were necessary everywhere. Riding the circuit brought the priest into contact with isolated Catholics whose normal contact with the Church, if any, was through catechists.

On an ordinary trip around the circuit, the visiting priest would spend his time at each outstation inquiring after the spiritual and material condition of the Christian families, consulting with the local catechist and the head Christian, and making friends with the children. About five o'clock, the missionary would eat his rice and, if there were any women who wanted to confess their sins, he would hear their confessions in order to comply with the regulation that confessions of women be heard before sundown to avoid grounds for scandal. Following the celebration of Mass in the morning, the priest would move on if the number of Christians in the village was small and there was no priest's residence. Some of the priests, such as the Maryknoller Murray in the Pingnan, Guangxi, district, used their circuit riding to successfully introduce Western medicine into the countryside.[4]

The Role of the Sisters and the Lay Mission Workers

Valuable church workers in addition to the priests were the American and European Catholic Sisters recruited by priests to do dispensary and educational work in the missions. Some of the Sisters also taught catechism, cared for orphans, and organized sisterhoods of Chinese women. Their educational work for girls was an important contribution to Chinese social development. The Sisters' dispensary work, for which they charged at most a copper coin or two, brought Western medicine to millions of Chinese who otherwise could not have afforded it. In 1935-36 alone, their seventy-one dispensaries treated more than 450,000 patients.[5]

The teachers in the Catholic mission networks, whether priests, Sisters, Brothers, catechists, or ordinary pedagogues, were another force for change in the Chinese hinterland. The peasantry and townspeople were eager to have their sons educated. The eagerness sometimes developed into healthy rivalry. Vincentians in the Ganzhou area found that their establishment of a new school in Sha Da moved neighboring villages to establish their own schools. The Vincentians broke some barriers by providing both girls' schools and coeducational schools in addition to boys' schools. Where financial considerations prevented the missionaries from establishing a school, they subsidized the work of a traditional village schoolteacher. By 1935 American Catholic missionaries were operating more than seventy rudimentary schools, 550 primary schools, and five high schools. About 10,000 boys and 5000 girls, Christian and non-Christian, attended the schools.[6]

The most important Chinese employees of the missions were the catechists. They represented the Church to both Christians and non-Christians where there was no resident priest. At mission stations with a resident priest, the catechists worked under his supervision to instruct catechumens. Along with catechism lessons, they provided rudimentary language instruction for the generally illiterate peasants. Because Chinese custom forbade the instruction of women by men, male catechists instructed only men and left the instruction of women, including their own wives, to female catechists and to members of the Catholic sisterhoods.

Though many of the missionaries depended upon the catechists to communicate with the Chinese and to provide needed information about local events and politics, some of the foreigners were unhappy with the catechists. One of their more severe critics, who recognized their importance to church work, labeled them "mercenary troops" and complained, "Now in the face of an obstacle what does the catechist do? The best of them walk right up against it, and then lay down right in front of it." The critical Maryknoller explained, "Of course, it gets down to psychology, after all, and no one blames the catechist. He is Chinese, that's all. The Chinese has his gifts, but he is not the man to take the message to Garcia. The first thing he will do is to ask you, 'Where is Garcia at?', and then he will want a special train to get there. He must have the foreigner at his back."[7]

Training Native Cadres

As far as the Vatican was concerned, the relationship of the foreign missionaries to Chinese Catholics was most critical in the area of cadre development: the training of Chinese priests by the missionaries. The Americans trained seminarians only to the high school stage; college-level training of Chinese seminarians remained under the control of European missionaries.

The Americans put much effort into their work at the preparatory seminary level. The American Franciscans, for example, opened St. Anthony Minor Seminary in Wuchang in 1923 and another at Huangshigang, Laohutou, in 1924. By 1935 the American Catholics were operating a dozen minor seminaries with 407 students. Twenty-eight graduates from their preparatory seminaries were pursuing advanced training for the Catholic priesthood.[8]

American priests enjoyed much better relations with their pupils than did the European seminary directors and teachers.[9] That the preparatory seminarians were so far from ordination, that so few of them progressed from the minor to the major seminary, and that fewer still persevered to become priests muted the tensions that otherwise would have arisen between the American and potential Chinese competitors for their jobs.

The high attrition among Chinese seminarians was due to various factors: the requirement of celibacy which undermined family security without providing the family anything comparable in return; the need to master both classical Western and Chinese secular studies as well as Thomistic philosophy and Catholic theology; and the years of grinding subservience to European teachers.[10]

Failing to Crusade against Protestantism

Busy with his organizational duties and the training of young cadres, the American Catholic missionary failed to develop his role as anti-Protestant crusader. The American Catholic generally had much better relations with Protestant missionaries in China than did European Catholics.[11] Among the American Catholics, the Maryknollers seem to have enjoyed the warmest personal ties with Protestant missionaries. One Maryknoller commented, "We will be glad to see the local Protestant mission again in active commission, for we feel that in Pagan lands Protestant Mission activity is helpful rather than a deterrent to our work. On the whole, the personal relations between priests and ministers have been very pleasant, and many a missionary priest has owed his continuance in rigorous work to the kindly ministration of Protestant Mission Doctors."[12]

American members of monastic groups were slower to put aside anti-Protestant feelings. The American Dominican leaders in Fujian, for example, attributed agrarian revolt in the province partly to the Protestant missionaries, who propagated "the old fallacy of personal inspiration." The Passionists in Hunan felt threatened by the manifold activities of their local Protestant counterparts, many of whom belonged to the German Evangelical Church. The Passionists believed that the Protestants preached against them and that their well-funded charities overshadowed Catholic efforts. They determined to compete, but by 1926 financial stringency had forced the Passionists to put aside their ambitious plans to build an institutional network to rival that of the Protestants. The Passionists later developed friendly personal ties with the Protestants.[13]

Anti-Protestantism was not a sentiment likely to survive the growing Chinese nationalism which lumped all foreign missionaries together as enemies. Although Catholic missionaries knew that the antiforeign events of the mid-1920s were forcing Protestant missionaries from China, they were so preoccupied with their own survival and the protection of their institutions that any crusading sentiments vanished. A few years before, the Passionists' magazine had trumpeted: "Whether or no China shall become a child of the Church or a fruitful field of Protestantism will depend in the main on the spirit shown by American Catholics toward this great work, the preaching of the Gospel in China."[14] Now the Catholic missionaries began to worry more about their own safety than about Protestant activity. In November 1924, a Vincentian writing from Jiangxi likened the atmosphere to that preceding the Boxer Uprising at the turn of the century.[15]

Persons with a Few Stammered Words

The antiforeignism spreading through China was fed in part by the linguistically deficient and socially clumsy missionaries, by envy of their relative wealth, and by resentment aroused by their privilege and power.

The failure of most missionaries to master Chinese handicapped the Catholic Church and evoked resentment from many Chinese. The biographer of F. X. Ford, head of the Mei Xian (Kaying) mission, noted that Ford was unable to communicate properly with his followers because he never learned Hakka well. Theophane Maguire, writing of his days in the Passionists' Hunan mission, observed that the Passionists' inability to master the Chinese language as well as their social awkwardness were obstacles to the progress of the Church. Even Catholics found these deficiencies hard to bear. The Chinese Catholics in one Guangdong village were so disgusted when a bumbling, stuttering Maryknoller replaced the resident Chinese priest that they refused to accept the American.[16]

The linguistic limitations of the American Catholics can be traced to a lack of formal instruction in the language. Not until the late 1930s did some American missionaries undertake a formal course of language instruction available in Beijing especially for Catholic missionaries. Generally, the local course of instruction was conducted as circumstances permitted. In the Mei Xian mission, newcomers were handed a Hakka dictionary compiled by the Maryknoller Drought and were sent off to their station in the company of a catechist who spoke no English.[17] Elsewhere, the presence of fellow English speakers distracted the Americans from their language study. Almost everywhere at least some pastoral duties interfered with learning Chinese.

Persons of Wealth

The conspicuous wealth of the missionaries made the Chinese envious and suspicious of the motives of the missionaries, and aroused misgivings in a few of the churchpeople. That wealth also attracted a Chinese following whose integrity the missionaries questioned but whose presence they needed to justify their missionary role.

The missionary lifestyle was far above that of the average Chinese. An American Vincentian wrote from Jiangxi, "Of late, I have been making a tour of our territory, giving missions. During these tours, we live in the homes of the Christians and eat their food. I can vouch for it; there is a vast difference between conditions and food as found in the priests' residence and in their [the Chinese] homes."[18]

Some missionaries felt besieged by the poor. In Baojing, Hunan, the Passionist priest, Raphael Vance, became convinced that avarice was the main characteristic of the Chinese. Landowners had tried to gouge him; workmen at the mission had struck for higher wages; the catechist and some Christians had tried to rob him, he charged in a letter which warned that the country was ripe for "Soviet Revolution." Later he found that his best catechist was supporting a mistress with food and money stolen from the mission. Another catechist stole $400 from a woman and ran off to join the bandits.[19]

Even Chinese Christians sometimes found it hard to see the missionary as other than a mercenary. After completing a tour of the region south of Maoming, Guangdong, in the spring of 1922, Bernard F. Meyer reported of the entire area that "almost all the world suspects and fears, if it does not hate you! Many of your own Christians do not as yet fully grasp the motives that brought you here. Some of them seem to think that they have done you a favor by becoming Christians."[20]

Although an occasional missionary expressed misgivings about the relatively luxurious lifestyle the Western church workers enjoyed, few turned their backs on the example of their European predecessors, who insisted on at least a modicum of comfort. Enjoying the warmth of two oil stoves on a cold, damp January day in 1921, the Maryknoll missionary at Wuzhou (Wuchow) wrote in the mission chronicle, "Thanks to John D's zeal in pushing his interests, we secured two oil stoves. It was hard to enjoy them, though, when you thought of the poor Chinese who could not afford such luxury." The chronicler, who had three house servants, could perhaps have salved his conscience by recalling the advice of Monsignor de Guebriant to the Americans: "Your house must be comfortable; you are not Chinese and cannot live as they do. It must be your first consideration. Chapels and the like are secondary. If you do not have enough money for both, build a good house first, and let the chapel wait. Your health, and therefore your work depend upon it."[21]

Most missionaries viewed their resources not as personal emoluments but as a somewhat questionable means of attracting the poor. Fearful that scattered Chinese Catholics would abandon their religion, the Maryknoller Bernard F. Meyer, for example, proposed to buy enough land near Dongzhen, Guangdong, to settle a hundred or more persons, and to build a chapel and boys' and girls' schools. Meyer said he would keep the schools filled by threatening parents with eviction from the community and its scarce rice fields if their children failed to attend classes. Given the economics of the Guangdong scene, he wrote, it was "comparatively easy to bring people to the Church—$50 a head and good interest on the money, with land rising in value." He foresaw that such converts would be labeled "rice Christians," but in defense of his plan he wrote, "Of course, getting a living would attract them at the beginning but I shall call that a 'beginning of faith' that would remove prejudice and lead them to give their minds to the study of truth. With what trembling knees the most of them approach the priest for the first time."[22]

Although Meyer did not realize his plan in Guangdong, other Catholic missionaries accomplished similar plans in North China. In so doing, they underscored the connection between capital and power on the local level in China. The ability to buy and distribute land to selected needy individuals gave that person or institution immense local power. When not allocating land itself, the Church often distributed the fruits of the land to catechumens. This practice resulted in fewer "rice Christians" than in what might be termed "rice catechumens." One Maryknoller in Luoding, Guangdong, wrote, "When they saw that somebody was spending money, they began to flock in droves." He consoled himself with the idea that there were "ways of telling the sheep from the goats, and it is much better than not creating any interest at all."[23]

The story was much the same in Hunan, where the Passionist Fathers worked. Paul Ubinger discovered that many Catholics entered the Church "simply for the sake of bodily protection, temporal goods or financial assistance." Once admitted to church membership, they abandoned study of the catechism, apostasized, married polygamously, took concubines or became opium dealers or addicts. Ubinger wrote of the results: "It is a most difficult task to be obliged to convert the supposed to be Christians before converting the pagans. My missions have no good examples among the Christians to attract the pagans to the Church."[24]

Persons of Power

To offset missionary frustrations with the difficult language and customs as well as backsliding converts, the China missions offered freedom from conventual life and seminary routine, the mystique of an education far superior to that of one's parishioners and converts, and the backing of foreign powers. The Catholic mission pastor, in the words of the Vincentian Corbett, "runs his own house, directs and orders all things as he wishes—and has more liberty of action than any man in his wildest dreams can imagine back home. His people cling to him as the old Irish adhered to his 'Rivrence'—as our own fathers did to their pastors when to be a Catholic meant ostracism in many parts of Admiral Heflin's Patria Bombastica then as now." "The priest," Corbett went on, "is the pastor of his flock, the town doctor, lawyer—he is recognized as the brains of the village and he is supposed to know everything from hens to moonshine."[25]

Occasionally, missionaries played forceful roles made possible by their privileged status. After his arrival in Longnan, Jiangxi, Daniel McGillicuddy not only constantly raided opium dens but also smashed idols in the homes of nominal Catholics, literally terrorizing the townspeople in what a Vincentian confrere described as "a fight to the finish with the devil and his agents." The Vincentians John A. O'Shea and George V. Erbe also took vigorous measures against the use of opium by Catholics, and according to a confrere, "injected some militaristic Christianity just where it was needed and when it was needed."[26]

In this sort of behavior as well as in the organization of church work and in the enjoyment of wealth, the American Catholics copied their European predecessors. Foreign tutors and Chinese assistants quickly taught the tyro Americans not only how to carry out routine pastoral duties and to maintain a certain style of life, but also how to behave as men of power with the Chinese. Becoming a foreign missionary meant casting aside any democratic leanings and allowing personal prejudices free play. Thus shortly after his arrival in China, a young Maryknoller wrote from Guangzhou: "Of course the French are noted for their courtesy, but with a difference. They are not as democratic as we, they draw class distinctions more sharply. For example, I learned the Chinese word for 'thanks' the other day and proudly sprung it on the Chink who brought my laundry. I was at once corrected by one of the [French] Fathers, 'We never say that to the Chinese, it is only for equals.' "[27]

The French taught the newly arrived Americans that they had to behave as men of power and influence if they were to maintain their following. Soon after reaching China, the first group of Maryknollers signed a letter to a district magistrate asking that he protect local catechumens from pirates. Requested by the catechumens and drawn up by their French supervisor, the letter was a manifestation of the patronage essential to the survival of the Catholic Church in China. As Maryknoll co-founder Thomas F. Price wrote of the incident, "most of these people come to us and put themselves under instruction because they think the priest and the Church will protect them."[28]

Patronage implied more than protection. When a village of former Catholics sought the protection of the Maryknoll missionary in the Haiyan area of coastal Guangdong province, the priest, George Bauer, required that they return to regular observance of church law, that their elders and children show deference to the priest and to the catechist as well, and that the children attend school and catechism classes. In return, the priest promised not only protection and inexpensive brides from among the girls at the church orphanages in Haiyan and Yangjiang but also "that the children would have the best education in the whole region and so might easily become merchants and officials. Perhaps they might even become priests and bishops, as their former pastor, Father Yeung, had succeeded in becoming."[29]

To carry out their role in all its dimensions, the missionaries found it necessary to engage in a wide spectrum of political activity. At the town or village level, that meant cultivating landlords, petty officials, and other influentials. Thus when the Maryknollers, James E. Walsh and William F. O'Shea, arrived in Maoming, Guangdong, they carefully maintained the good relations with the local "upper crust" which their French predecessor, Joseph Antoine Mollat, had enjoyed. To have done otherwise would have been disastrous for the Church in Maoming; the Church was built upon the faith which Chinese of the most destitute sort had in the person and political influence of Mollat. As was often the case, a Chinese catechist carefully guided the inexperienced Americans through the social and political rituals of their role as patrons.[30]

The relative freedom of action, enhanced social standing, and sense of power the missionaries enjoyed were alluring, and the pursuit of them left a deep mark on the American Catholic missions in South China and elsewhere. Corbett remarked of the Vincentians in China, "In a year he is shifting for himself, if he so wishes and proves his ability. That is a strange thing—

almost every man wants a place to call his own." The same desire permeated the ranks of the Maryknoll missionaries in China and at home, with the result that the fast-growing Maryknoll Society snapped up already developed mission territories and avoided cultivation of much of the territory under its jurisdiction. After entering the Jiangmen mission in late 1918, the Maryknollers entered the Wuzhou, Guangxi, mission in 1920 and the Mei Xian, Guangdong, mission in 1924. Of the move into Guangxi, the Maryknoll leader in China commented that it promised "more esprit de corps, more corporate influence, and more of many other things." Supporting the subsequent move into Mei Xian he noted, "The situation is that even with our new territory in the Kongmoon [Jiangmen] Prefecture we haven't got enough missions just now to give all our possible pastors all a place." Admitting that the move into Mei Xian would put off further into the future the development of "poor old Kwangsi [Guangxi]," he felt that was inevitable anyway for the society had few men capable of doing the hard work of breaking new ground in Guangxi. Groundbreaking in such areas was "not by nature pressing." Furthermore, he argued, by taking over established missions the Maryknoll Society would save at least $25,000, the cost of a building program "which we would soon have to engage in to accommodate our men."[31]

Without men who could open new missions, without money to build new central mission stations, and without any other way to retain its high-spirited membership or attract energetic new members, the Maryknoll organization embarked on a frenzied policy of expansion in China and beyond. The expansion was designed to provide mission pastorates for the priests graduating yearly from its seminary. It opened new missions in the Pyong Yang vicariate, Korea, 1923; Honolulu diocese, Hawaii, 1926; Fushun vicariate, Manchuria, 1932; Kyoto, Japan, 1934. These areas provided the openings for the society's active missionaries who numbered twenty in 1923, thirty-seven in 1925, sixty in 1927, 106 in 1931, and 225 in 1941. The Maryknoll Society became the chief religious link of American Catholicism to the non-Christian world beyond the United States and maintained a vigorous momentum until it was caught between anticolonialism abroad and anti-imperialism and anti-authoritarianism at home. Those forces pared and honed the society into an intellectual and moral cutting edge of the American Catholic Church in the United States.

In China, however, the Maryknoll Society fitted easily into an institution that the wealthy perceived as both competitor and ally against the multitudes of poor. The Maryknollers in strife-torn Guangdong believed that the wealthy were friendly to them and other foreign priests because the wealthy realized "that their best tenants [were] Christians and that Christianity was their safest bulwark against the ever threatening 'chaaks' or banditry," people who were in Maryknoll eyes "hunger crazed" peasants stricken by drought, floods, and plague.[32]

Comfortable with the Status Quo

The Guangdong landlords were correct in their assessment that the missionaries did not plan to push for any sweeping social reforms or revolutions. Indeed, American Catholic missionaries had little sympathy for any reform of Chinese society, except perhaps for the introduction of universal education, the prohibition of infanticide, and freedom for women to choose their spouses. The Maryknoller F. X. Ford, for example, faulted Protestant missionaries who sought to improve social conditions in China and labeled them fanatics. He believed that what he saw as the downward course of Protestantism in China and in the United States was traceable to the presence of so many lay church employees working to reform society. In his eyes, the 400 ordained Presbyterian ministers in China were not enough to "christianize the bustling activities of their one thousand co-workers which had degenerated into a materialistic philosophy." The same priest also took exception to the YMCA's special prominence "in popular lectures on delicate subjects," among which was contraception.[33]

Unwilling to change the status quo which favored them so greatly, and upset by the reform efforts of Western Protestants, the American Catholics did not credit the Chinese with the capacity to change their own society. The Maryknoller Daniel O'Shea, for example, found some very mean cases of oppression in Guangdong, professed not to know what could be done, and added, "C'est la Chine! And when they [the Chinese] have had Christ for two thousand years we will have a right to expect better from them."[34]

However comfortable the missionaries were with the status quo, a wild swirl of forces was changing China. Often enjoying foreign backing, regional warlords vied for national power. Their destructive campaigns were supported by exactions from the wealthy, who in turn gouged the already oppressed peasants and workers. The nation's youth turned against the militarists and through the vehicles of the Nationalist and Communist parties began antiforeign and antiwarlord campaigns that slowly grew into a national movement of enormous strength. Simultaneously, some of the young ventured into the countryside, where they found millions of peasants disaffected from the agrarian order.

The Violent Erosion of the Missionaries' Power

As nationalism and antiforeignism grew in strength, church people found that they no longer could count upon the deference of the Chinese; only naked power could protect them in turbulent local circumstances. Thus although missionaries occasionally functioned as mediators between warring militarists and invariably opened their missions to refugees, the proximity of foreign military forces seems to have determined the security of the mission compounds. In June 1921, for example, when refugees crowded into the

Wuzhou mission compound to escape strife between the soldiers of Guangdong and Guangxi, the presence of the U.S.S. *Pampanga* guaranteed the inviolability of the Maryknoll mission. When the Guangdong and Guangxi troops fought over Maoming shortly thereafter without nearby American forces, the mediation efforts of Bernard Meyer broke down, the mission was invaded, and the priests and refugees were robbed. Similarly, in January 1925, at Nan'anfu, Jiangxi, the Vincentian Thomas Crossley was unable to prevent rampaging troops from invading his compound and looting those who had taken refuge there.[35]

Where foreign force was not evident, missionaries began to notice Chinese hostility toward them. In northwestern Hunan, the Passionist superior Dominic Langenbacher lamented as early as 1923 that the local people were drawing no distinction between the missionaries and "agents of aggressive governments or of grasping commercial houses." Not long thereafter, in January 1924, soldiers of General He Jian's First Hunan Divison appeared at the Xupu, Hunan, mission, trained their rifles on Fathers Flavian Mullins and Arthur Benson, opened fire and slightly wounded Mullins. After claiming that "Americans were anxious to take China and make the Chinese slaves," they fired on the American flag and vandalized the mission. They left when an officer appeared and ordered them away.[36]

The Passionists immediately moved to invoke American governmental assistance and so shore up their position in Xupu. Mullins, a source of valuable military information to the American government, lodged a complaint with the American consul at Changsha, Hunan. If reparations weren't made, he argued, "America and Americans will not have the respect of even the local Chinese." The American vice-consul at Changsha, Mr. Meinhardt, represented the matter to the commander-in-chief of the Hunanese forces, Gen. Zhao Hengdi. Although the soldiers involved went unpunished, the priests received $1000 from Chinese authorities. The governor of Hunan and the Chinese government both tendered apologies.[37]

Nonetheless, the position of the Americans in isolated northwestern Hunan continued to deteriorate. In December 1924, bandits robbed two Passionists and the five recently arrived Sisters of Charity whom they were accompanying on the Yuan River to Yuanling. Troubled conditions prevented the Sisters from reaching their destination until early July 1925, after three attempts to do so. By then bandits had burned out the little mission station of Lao Zi Cheng. About the same time the Sisters arrived in Yuanling, soldiers looted Fr. Theophane Maguire's Yongsui mission, the center of extensive dispensary work among the local Miao tribespeople.[38]

Antiforeignism was also increasing among the peasantry elsewhere in South China and undercut the Church's position by eroding its wealth and its ability to exercise effective power. In Fujian, from 1923 onward, the vicar apostolic of Fuzhou, Monsignor Aguirre, found it impossible to collect rents on his extensive farm and timber land because the peasants had organized a rent strike.[39]

Popular antiforeignism made it increasingly difficult for local influentials to cooperate with the missionaries. In late 1924, Yuanling civic leaders approached the Passionists for a two-month loan of $12,000 to put toward a ransom of $80,000 demanded by a militarist in return for sparing the city. Because some of the military officers were friends of the priests, the missionaries confidently refused the request for a loan. Instead, they offered to buy public property which lay behind the mission and which under normal circumstances would not have been sold to foreigners. As the Passionist superior, Langenbacher, wrote, "Only at such a time of trouble as this, can we hope to get it." Outraged and deeply fearful of popular reaction, the civic leaders turned down the Americans' offer.[40]

Fear of popular antiforeignism affected even provincial authorities. In 1925, Maryknoll priests in Guangdong tried to buy some government-owned wasteland across the Jiangmen River from Jiangmen City. The Maryknoll superior, James E. Walsh, in full compliance with the various Chinese and American legal requirements under the terms of the Chinese-American Treaty of 1903, purchased about twenty acres from the Guangdong government. The Guangdong government reneged on the sale because it feared the political repercussions of selling public land to foreigners. Antiforeign sentiment was then at fever pitch as a result of the slaughter of Chinese demonstrators by foreign police in Shanghai (May 30) and other cities. The Jiangmen mission district thus lost the sum of its liquid capital and failed in its first attempt to buy land under the terms of the Sino-American Treaty, rather than under the terms of the Franco-Chinese treaties. The American government was unable to provide any immediate relief to the aggrieved missionaries and the issue dragged on for years until the Guangdong government made partial restitution. The Maryknollers received land at the mouth of the Jiangmen River, where they built a leprosorium.[41]

The Jiangmen land affair was one of the lesser manifestations of the strong Chinese reaction to the murder of Chinese demonstrators by British police forces in late May 1925. The Maryknoll leader in South China compared the widespread antiforeign demonstrations and strikes that followed the incident to the Boxer Uprising itself. On the advice of the American consul and a French bishop, he recalled his mission personnel to Hong Kong and all but four priests and a Brother managed to reach the British colony. They found Hong Kong to be unsafe, but the priests were unable to return to the still more dangerous interior until October 1925, and the Sisters waited even longer before returning. Meanwhile, their leader lamented that Russian Communists and Chinese political leaders with axes to grind were easily duping workers and students (the latter, "the most irresponsible and generally idiotic element in China") by dragging the red herring of "the poor old foreigner" across the trail. He felt that the Chinese badly needed a "spanking" by the foreign nations because of their "ridiculous tactics," but acknowledged that such a course of action would make the interior totally unsafe for foreigners for a long time. His sentiments reflected the shrinkage of foreign power in China. That power would shrink still further as Chinese nationalism assumed an organized, military form, eventually threatening the existence of all foreign missions.[42]

4

Militant Nationalism and the
First Collapse of the Missions

The foreign presence in China was thin and fragile; its weakest and most exposed element was the missionary activity. Beyond the range of the gunboats, attracting the envy of Christian and non-Christian alike by their life-style, the missionaries were certain to draw attacks from antiforeign Chinese. Those attacks would rain upon missionary groups divided by institutional and national rivalries and hard pressed to maintain the image of enterprises riding out passing political squalls. Though the missionaries would not be able to intimidate the Chinese, mission propagandists in the United States did manage to hide the fury of the Nationalists from American Catholics and lay the seeds for future misunderstanding of the China scene.

The Nationalist Party Spearheads Chinese Antiforeignism

The popular outbreaks of the May 30 Movement were a prelude to the more effective antiforeignism of the Chinese Nationalist Party under the leadership of Jiang Jieshi (Chiang Kai-shek). After the death of Sun Yixian (Sun Yat-sen) in March 1925, Jiang waited only until July 1 to proclaim the establishment of a nationalist government. Within six months he had control of Guangdong and Guangxi and by July 1926 he was leading an expedition north to reunify a nation split into five major areas by warlords. Nationalist and Communist party propagandists preaching a heady gospel of antiworlordism, antiforeignism, and anti-Christianism preceded the 90,000 Nationalist troops who marched north from Guangzhou and Shantou (Swatow) on three fronts.

Thousands of missionaries, mostly Protestant, fled before the onslaught. Those who stayed suffered; a few died. The expeditionary forces and their allies damaged churches and schools and intimidated Chinese Christians. The rout of the foreign church people fed the confidence of the nationalists and stripped the foreigners of their aura of power.

The response of the foreign powers was to evacuate their nationals wherever possible and to increase their military forces in China. The leadership of the Roman Catholic Church, on the other hand, decided to keep its missionaries in China and to discourage them from seeking reparations for damages suffered at the hands of the Chinese. It also put aside deference to European nations and amidst great publicity consecrated six Chinese priests as bishops.

The Vatican's gesture in consecrating Chinese priests as bishops may have alleviated some of the discontent of Chinese priests, who increased from 400 at the turn of the century to 1369 in 1929. It did not, however, deflect much of the animosity that permeated the country.

Militant Chinese Nationalism Strikes the American Catholic Missions

The tension between missionary and non-Christian was greater than that between missionary and Christian Chinese, so much greater that it flashed into violence. At Fuzhou, Fujian, in mid-January 1927, rioters destroyed the Spanish mission and in late March the populace of Huazhou (Fachow), Guangdong, sacked the Maryknoll mission in that town.

Both the official and the Maryknoll versions of the Huazhou incident indicate a lack of sympathy for the mission and the presence of many persons hostile to the foreign enterprise. According to the local magistrate, a church employee had refused to allow a soldier to dry his coat on the river bank in front of the church. When the soldier persisted, the employee threw a stone and injured the soldier. Then 300 to 400 people destroyed the church. The magistrate claimed that there was no proof of looting and that he could not reimburse the missionaries for damages resulting from "the indignation of an ignorant crowd." The Maryknoll leader in South China accused the Huazhou magistrate of consistent hostility toward the mission. He blamed the affair on soldiers who had recently arrived from Meilu, where they had lived in the forcibly occupied mission. The soldiers had stoned the Maryknoll missioners in Huazhou, vandalized the church, and then allowed civilian looters to complete the destruction. He admitted, however, that the people of Huazhou showed no indignation over the affair.[1]

So intense was the antimissionary feeling in coastal Guangdong that armed troops were unnecessary to cause trouble. In the China missionary annals, Xiachuan (Sancian) was a symbol of zeal for the conversion of China. Here the famous Jesuit missionary and founding member of the Society of Jesus, Francis Xavier, had died before he could begin the proselytization of China. Xiachuan was under the ecclesiastical jurisdiction of the Jiangmen mission; when Rome made the Jiangmen mission a vicariate apostolic and consecrated James E. Walsh to be its vicar apostolic or bishop, Walsh chose the mission station at Xiachuan as the site of his consecration (May 22, 1926). In these years, however, Xiachuan was a symbol of civilian Chinese antiforeignism and anti-Christianism.

The church on Xiachuan was an institution battered by forces beyond its control. As a landlord it found that it could not collect monies due to the mission's Burial and Aid Societies; nor could it collect any rent on the 100 mou (seventeen acres) of rice land that it owned. The tenants refused payment even though the rent, ten percent of the harvest, was one-seventh the rate charged by neighboring landlords. Furthermore, the local people made a habit of stealing from the mission's woodlot rather than walk to the other side of the island for wood. The local missionary, Constantine F. Burns, considered it impossible to seek redress at law because the political situation was so unfavorable. His Chinese supporters concurred.[2]

Bled from without, the church on Xiachuan was hemmorhaging from within. Fifteen years after a period of mass conversions, the island had only 100 practicing Catholics. Among the 1300 nominal Catholics were a dozen or so bigamists. A dozen Christians had married without regard to ecclesiastical regulations or liturgy. Errant Christians reviled the catechists who rebuked them. The children of the Catholics told a French priest returning for a visit that Mass and the sacraments were no longer necessary. Almost all of the Catholics participated in the full range of New Year observances, including those the missionary found "un-Christian," such as the burning of incense. A former catechist publicly apostasized "with all the accompanying ceremonies of placating the devil and welcoming back heathen gods. A Buddhist priest performed."[3]

Not long after the Xiachuan catechist's public apostasy, the anti-Christianism of the nationalist movement made a dramatic entrance. A man who had studied medicine at Guangzhou's French hospital returned to Xiachuan with his wife. The woman's first act when "she put foot on the beach across from the [priest's] house was to raise her fist in defiance of the Church and denounce in bitter terms the religion of the foreigners," reported Burns. To him they both seemed steeped in Bolshevism and anti-Christianity.[4]

The tide of antiforeignism and anti-Christianism skirted the Hakka country in mountainous northern Guangdong, leaving the Mei Xian mission relatively undisturbed, but it broke with full force against the Dominican mission. They also took over the stations in Jianyang and Songxi. In the Nationalist soldiers took over the Dominicans' Jian'ou mission, hectored the priests and their servants, and stole furniture and building materials from the mission. They also took over the stations in Jianyang and Songxi. In the small villages, the local populace seized mission property. The Dominicans departed.[5]

Nationalism plagued the Wuchang mission for months. Nationalist propagandists and agitators accused the Franciscan missionaries of being political spies, foreign emissaries, and forerunners of commercial and military invasions. In October 1926, Nationalist troops seized Wuchang and invaded the mission compound there, later making off with $3000 worth of valuables from the seminary. In December, Communist agitators instigated a strike against the Wuchang mission and were able to prevent most public celebrations of Christmas. Antimission propaganda claiming that the Catholics were digging out the eyes of babies forced Fr. Leo Ferrary to close his Wuchang dispensary. The soldier also seized the Wuchang mission high school and turned it into a military cadet school and occupied the church and Sisters' convent just outside Wuchang. In Xianning and in the country area, the militant Farmers Union seized the Franciscans' property. In Huangshi 200 soldiers occupied the convent, school and hospital. In the Wuchang territory, mission work stopped.[6]

Other missions were closed by the Nationalists. The Sisters of Loretto were forced to halt their work in Wuhan during April 1927, as were the Sisters of Providence in Kaifeng.[7]

The Nationalists' vanguard did not exploit the divisions between the missionaries and the Chinese laity as they did the divisions between the missionaries and the non-Christian Chinese. In fact, heavy-handed bullying by vanguard forces drove the laity to rally around the missionaries, thereby momentarily strengthening the Church. Events in the Ganzhou vicariate illustrate this process.

As late as May 1926, the American Vincentians in the Ganzhou vicariate had felt secure, but the approach of the Northern Expedition's central column changed all of that. The antiforeign and antireligious spirit was growing stronger. Agitators in the Nationalist vanguard threatened and insulted the missionaries. They bullied the catechumens, nearly emptying the mission schools. In November the Nationalists encouraged a mob that marched on the Ganzhou mission hospital and would have destroyed it, had the local chamber of commerce supported the action. The Nationalists denied Catholics membership in the Nationalist Party and even in the workmen's guilds. All workmen were required to belong to a guild in order to earn a living, and Catholics were told publicly to apostasize and publish their apostasy on three successive days in the local press in order to gain guild membership.[8]

The Nationalists maintained their pressure on the Church and on Chinese Catholics with agents in every marketplace propagandizing against the Church. In Ganzhou they injected antichurch propaganda into the massive demonstrations held two or three times each week. Some of the demonstrators staged a mock confession scene; rain washed out a planned mock Mass. The three daily newspapers published what one Vincentian termed "calumnies against the Church that would be worthy of Nero and the tyrants of ancient Rome." Through it all the priests, as one of them put it, "had absolutely no human consolation to offer the Christians."[9]

The Christians resisted. Under the pressure only fifteen of the vicariate's 15,000 Catholics apostasized. In fact, in most places in the vicariate,

Catholics were anxious to fight those who reviled the Catholic Church and them. But the bishop ordered the missionaries to prevent fighting "at all costs" and the priests restrained them. The decision was wise, for the militant Catholics were no match for the well-disciplined Cantonese troops who moved into Ganzhou, took over mission chapels and schools, and destroyed crucifixes and holy pictures to emphasize their hatred of Christianity.[10]

Although the presence of the troops paralyzed mission work, the missionaries were in no hurry to see the Nationalists leave the mission stations. The troops were well-behaved and their presence was a protection against the street mobs gathered by the Nationalist agents whose anti-Christian line was so successful that local Christians decided to forgo any public celebration of Christmas.[11]

In the Yuanling territory in northwestern Hunan, an area whose uplands were heavily populated by Miao tribespeople, the tactics of the Nationalist vanguard were also counterproductive. In the outlying areas the Nationalists met resistance from the Miao because they wore western clothing, something which the Miao found offensive, whereas the resident missionary Passionists, in Yongsui at least, had tried to adopt local ways and had helped many thousands of Miao to survive a terrible famine earlier in the year. But in the cities, the Nationalists were far more successful and forced the Catholic schools in Yuanling to march their students in political parades. In the turbulent atmosphere of Yuanling, the Passionists' mission was able to survive in large part because of the influence of the friendly Gen. Zen Youmou, an old friend of the missioners and a power in western Hunan.[12]

The missionaries who found the soldiery to be some protection against mob violence soon learned that the Nationalist government intended to regulate the mission schools. On January 23, 1927, the same day a proclamation appeared in Yuanling from Jiang Jieshi deprecating the extremes of the propagandists and agitators, the Nationalists' new educational regulations reached the Passionists. Jiang's picture was to be hung in every classroom; religion courses, formerly required, were reduced to an elective; the Nationalist doctrine was to be taught and all teachers hired and fired through the local board of education; school principals and the majority of school boards were to be Chinese. The priests felt that they would not be able to teach the mission's orphans and seminarians as they felt they ought. "How can we baptize infants, if we cannot provide for their Christian upbringing?" the Passionist Cuthbert O'Gara asked. In his view, the Passionists had "passed into a new phase of the struggle."[13]

Because the mission schools were already in such disarray, the Nationalists' new school regulations had little immediate impact. But they did complicate the governance of high schools, as Catholic Sisters were to find in the Wuchang mission, and they did discourage the Dominicans in

Fujian from any secondary education work.[14] The regulations were an early warning of a coming struggle between church and state.

Many American Catholics Flee

The magnitude of the antiforeign wave which engulfed South and Central China from 1925 through 1927 prompted the foreign powers to recall their nationals from the interior and even from some of the treaty ports. The Jiangmen Maryknollers left their mission in 1925 on consular orders and returned only after many months. The Dominicans in Fujian left in early 1927, following the destruction of the Fuzhou mission. The Catholic Sisters in the Yuanling mission left on consular orders and the Passionist priests followed them in late April 1927. The priests soon returned to their posts ignorant of the ban on such a step issued by the Department of State. The American Franciscans at Wuchang abandoned their mission on orders of the American consul in Wuhan. When the Sisters of Loretto in Hanyang were slow to evacuate, the American consul threatened to send a company of Marines to evacuate them, willing or not. They left the next day for Shanghai.[15]

Although many Catholic missionaries waited in Shanghai and Hong Kong for the chance to return to their posts, some left China. The Sisters of Providence, for example, obeyed the orders of the American consul to leave Kaifeng and left for Beijing on April 9, 1927. When Beijing became unsafe, two of the Sisters went home to the United States and the others went to Korea, where they studied Chinese and taught English. In October, two more of their number returned to the United States and the remaining Sisters were not able to return to Kaifeng until April 1929. The Dominican provincial superior took advantage of the turmoil to bring four of his missionaries home from Jian'ou to raise funds. Predictably, the Europeans interpreted their departures as a sign of cowardice.[16]

During this period of militant Chinese nationalism, the American Dominicans developed a bitter resentment toward their own government and its consul in Fuzhou. One of the central issues involved the Nationalist government's "Provisional Regulations Governing Property Acquired by Foreign Missions in the Interior." Although Washington had protested to the Nanjing government that these regulations infringed on American treaty rights, the Dominicans found that the American consul in Fuzhou advocated submission to Chinese regulations. The consul was also reluctant to encourage their complaints against Chinese officials and citizens who were taking over Dominican mission stations and stealing mission property. The American priests therefore worked through the French consul and followed the more assertive French government's policy. Meagher, the Dominican provincial superior, wrote to an official of the (American) National Catholic Welfare

Conference, "The Chinese had the right to make their own laws but that we would tamely submit to such a confiscation is simply against the tradition of any nation that has any backbone whatever." Even though the French protests were fruitless, their vigor pleased the American Dominicans.[17]

The American government's concern, however, was protection of the lives of its nationals in China, and it showed its continuing willingness to use force. At Yangjiang on November 12, 1927, two Maryknoll priests were strolling among crowds that were celebrating Sun Yixian's birthday. One of the two Americans, Fr. Fletcher, "unwisely flicked a normal school student on the ankle with a cane when the student attempted in a deliberate and rude manner to pass between him and another priest while walking in the city." The student body and some workmen demanded an apology and attempted to break into the mission before the military quelled them and arrested several of the leaders. Meanwhile, at the suggestion of the local military authorities, who feared that the Guangdong authorities would not approve their defense of foreigners, Fr. Dietz sought help from the American consul. The U.S.S. *Asheville* was soon in Yangjiang. Because no Maryknollers had died in the affair, the vicar apostolic of Jiangmen was convinced that antiforeignism had begun to decline.[18]

Despite the gigantic antiforeign upheaval, it was still possible for at least one missionary leader to accord little significance to political developments. On January 30, 1927, the vicar apostolic of Jiangmen wrote, "I can assure you that there is no trouble in China except that made by Russia. The Chinese are the best people in the world. All the talk about 'national aspirations,' 'unequal treaties,' 'imperialism,' etc.—these are the only red herrings. I wish they were sincere; it might mean that the Chinese were taking an interest in their own country and thus promise for the future. But it is not the case. These are catchwords used by the Soviet, that is all."[19] For himself he remained more concerned with the finances of the mission than with the political situation.

Chinese Nationalism Further Complicates Missionary Finances

Financing the missions was indeed a major problem, made more difficult by intra-Church rivalry and by Chinese antiforeignism. The American Dominicans experienced problems which exemplified those encountered by other groups. At the Chinese end of the financial network, the vicar apostolic of Fuzhou diverted to the use of local Chinese clergy funds received from American women for the American Dominicans in Fuzhou. At the American end of the network, the Dominicans found it impossible to enter the large eastern dioceses to seek contributions. In Boston, simply getting permission to enter the parochial schools to publicize the mission effort was difficult. Newark and, after mid-1927, Buffalo were two dioceses in which they could solicit alms. Even there, however, they found themselves competing not only with other missionary groups but with Propaganda Fide's fund-raising arm, the Society for the Propagation of the Faith. SPF set the not-very-generous rules for fund raising, for Propaganda Fide was determined to increase its share of monies collected for missionary work and thus increase its control over the missions.[20]

Ethnic rivalry threw up barriers to mission fund raisers that even organizational ties could not span. When Propaganda Fide transferred nineteen counties of the Jinan, Shandong province, mission from the German Franciscans to the American Franciscans, the Germans not only allowed operations in the new American area to run down, but also siphoned off into their own coffers funds coming from America for the American friars. These funds were hard-won because the American friars had found many parishes in the United States (including those run by their own St. Louis, Missouri province) closed to their appeals but open to those of the Germans.[21]

Even the Maryknoll Society was experiencing financial difficulties in 1926. Competition from other mission societies and a building program at home had cut into its funds. The Maryknollers' sense of economy seems to have weakened as construction progressed. The society suspended the building program but still had money problems because there were more people to feed and educate. Furthermore, the Maryknoll sisterhood had not reached economic self-sufficiency and threatened to burden the priests' society with debt should it collapse. In some places overseas, James A. Walsh believed, the priests had spoiled the Sisters by seeking to provide them with the comfort that the Sisters enjoyed at their Maryknoll motherhouse.[22]

Not content with what the Maryknoll Society could provide, the leader of the Jiangmen mission sought to jog the head of the (American) National Society for the Propagation of the Faith, Monsignor Quinn, into greater benevolence. The problem, however, was not with Quinn but with the local diocesan directors. Their attitude over the years, in the opinion of American and European Catholic missioners, had consistently been one of "patronizing contempt." Moreover, while the Maryknoll propaganda magazine, *Field Afar*, channeled money through SPF, SPF rarely received undesignated gifts and still more rarely passed along any of those monies to Maryknoll. They went instead to other groups. Nor had the American clergy done much for the Jiangmen mission. Only 323 American priests had ever sent money to the Jiangmen Maryknollers; most of the 323 were not pastors in the Catholic population centers of the Northeast and upper Midwest but "missionaries themselves in the middle west and west."[23]

To raise funds for the Jiangmen mission, its leader asked the head of the Maryknoll society to seek compensation for the looted Huazhou mission through the State Department. James A. Walsh replied that Vatican policy now was to discourage such action and that all requests for compensation had to be cleared with the Apostolic Delegate to China. For himself, he was "pleased to see that we are getting away from contact with American home government officials."[24]

The head of the Jiangmen mission had raised the matter of compensation, despite a warning that his society was not eager to capitalize on troubles in China. But he plunged ahead because his mission was still feeling the loss of its liquid capital in the Jiangmen land affair and of its station at Huazhou. The mission was also experiencing the strain of financing twenty-seven primary schools and twelve prayer schools. When he had previously written to James A. Walsh that the troubles in China were the "chance of a lifetime for propaganda" to raise money among the home folk, the master propagandist who headed the Maryknoll Society decided not to publicize the troubles. His own editorial policy for Maryknoll's *Field Afar* was "not to lament about present conditions," because "the whole Chinese situation in fact has had a tendency to make people question the value of spending money for missions in that country."[25]

James A. Walsh's observation that news of Chinese antiforeignism and mission losses was discouraging American Catholic contributions was correct. American Vincentians working in Ganzhou also found that the occupation of mission stations by Nationalist troops discouraged American benefactors.[26] Mission publicists had to work hard to persuade American Catholics that the China missions were fundamentally secure enterprises which generous and reasonable people should support. The propagandists succeeded well enough to generate support for the continuation of the mission and to recruit four more Catholic sisterhoods, one from Luxemburg and three from the American Midwest, an area with a surplus of Catholic Sisters.[27] That was the extent, however, of group voluntarism; lay financial support did not encourage any massive expansion of missionary activity in China.

Most of the missions were able to stagger back into activity and renew a broad institutional program. But looking into the future, F.X. Ford, leader of the Mei Xian mission, foresaw continuing economic and political difficulties. He therefore decided to forgo institutional work and concentrate instead on pastoral activity and the preparation of Chinese seminarians for the priesthood. Ford's fear of future troubles was justified. Jiang Jieshi's rapprochement with wealthy Chinese and with foreign powers split the Communists and the Nationalists and touched off another civil war that would not be resolved for two decades.

5

Civil War and Depression

From the establishment of the Chinese Nationalist government in Nanjing to the Chinese Communists' Long March which signaled the end of one stage of civil war between Nationalists and Communists, the American Catholic missions experienced major setbacks. Both sides in the war disrupted missionary activity and inflicted extensive damage on church institutions. In Jiangxi, Fujian, and Hunan provinces the Catholic Church suffered especially heavy losses. Clergy and laity were murdered, churches and schools destroyed, and church property handed over to the local populace. Moreover, Japan's armed seizure of Manchuria caused still further disruption of pastoral activities and damage to church property. In good times the losses would have been difficult to bear, but these were years of economic depression and that fact made the losses more grievous and recovery more difficult. Even where death and damage were not experienced, disruption of pastoral routine and delay of plans were commonplace. The morale of the missionaries sagged and the ardor of their supporters cooled.

The Uneven Impact of Civil Warfare

The civil war touched the missions in Guangxi and Guangdong either not at all or lightly. From 1928 through 1931, the activities of Communist irregulars and the Red Army complicated the work of the Maryknollers in the Mei Xian, Guangdong, mission. An unsuccessful Red Army attack upon Mei Xian on October 31, 1929, was the prelude to the looting of the Catholic mission at Shizheng the following day. Damage to the mission reached $2000. A return by the Communist forces in February 1930 cost only some of the resident missioner's clothing.[1] As a result of the troubled conditions, F.X. Ford delayed the foundation of a native teaching sisterhood. Ford eventually sidestepped the troubles by sending fourteen aspirants to the convent to Hong Kong where they trained under the direction of a Maryknoll Sister from 1930 to 1933.[2] These native Sisters were to strengthen the catechetical approach which was the salient feature of the Mei Xian mission under Ford's leadership.

Just over the border in Jiangxi, however, the American Vincentians of the Ganzhou vicariate apostolic experienced the full force of the civil war. Although the mission enjoyed a relatively peaceful 1928, it was stagnating because local Chinese remained convinced that Christians would soon suffer again. This pessimism was shaken neither by execution of a few Communists and bandits by Nationalist troops nor by the unprecedented gathering of all Jiangxi's officialdom and literati to celebrate John A. O'Shea's consecration as coadjutor bishop of Ganzhou on May 1, 1928. Adult conversions were less than half as numerous as two years before and the number of catechists had shrunken by a third.[3]

Aggressive Communist Enemies, Unfriendly Nationalist Allies

Events justified the fears of Ganzhou-area Chinese. Nine months after O'Shea's consecration, the Fourth Red Army led by Commander Zhu De and Party Representative Mao Zedong moved across Jiangxi on its way to Fujian province. As it marched, it singled out the Catholic Church for attack. On February 2, 1979, Mao and Zhu ordered the apprehension of Wang Ke'ai (Fr. Edward Young, C.M.). The order began with a preamble attacking the United States as an imperialistic country financing the reactionary Guomindang's (Nationalist Party) efforts to oppress Chinese laborers and peasants. The order further asserted that the United States was taking advantage of the missions and using them "as organs to further her interests by civilized exploitation of Chinese. These organs serve as vanguards of the capitalists and spies of imperialists." The order claimed that the Communists knew that laborers and peasants oppressed by Fr. Young, who allegedly was conspiring with "greedy and dishonest officials, local bullies, bad gentries, and militarists." Mao and Zhu further ordered a $10,000 ransom for Young to be distributed among the local workers and called for a distribution of the mission lands, the deportation of Young, and the permanent closure of the mission. The Communists charged that the mission kept the laborers and peasants from airing their grievances.[4]

Rashly believing that a foreigner backed by a powerful government could deter the Communists from attacking the Nan'an mission, Young attempted to return to that city and was taken prisoner by the Communists four miles from Nan'an on January 22, 1929. The Communists then looted the mission and demanded that the priest ask the vicar apostolic for $10,000 ransom. When Young refused, his captors threatened to execute him on the spot and then relented, perhaps, Young felt, because his show of bravery had touched the battle-hardened Red Army veterans. The soldiers, who numbered about 5000, marched Young off with them on January 24. To elude the

Nationalists they marched twenty-two hours a day and at one point when battle threatened momentarily they placed the privileged foreigner in their front line.

Since Young was far beyond the reach of American gunboats and blue-jackets, the American government used the Nationalist regime to rescue him. When Monsignor O'Shea contacted both the American consulate general in Wuhan and the (American) National Catholic Welfare Conference in Washington, he asked that the Nationalist government be pressured to send troops to rescue Young. The National Catholic Welfare Conference did in fact contact the State Department and ask it to represent the matter to the Chinese government in Nanjing. The Nationalists sent troops against the Communists who were holding Young, but Young's captors fled to avoid encirclement and allowed the priest to escape on January 27, 1929.[5]

The other Vincentians were more cautious than Young. Fr. William McClimont, for example, had fled his mission, a highly visible and beautiful white house with spacious grounds, five or six times in the previous two years, whenever there was any possible danger from bandits or Communists. He observed, "The greatest difficulty, in fact the only difficulty over here, is to face recurring disturbances ALONE."[6]

The Communists kept pressure on the Ganzhou vicariate apostolic. In March 1929, they looted and burned the missions at Xingguo and Anyuan. When the Red Army moved away, four bands of Communists remained behind; because of a split between the Guangxi and Nanjing regimes, no soldiers came to drive them off. The destruction continued into March 1929, when the mission stations at Nan'an, Xunwu, Ningdu, Ruijin, and Pinglu were reported looted and damaged.[7]

The situation produced a classic statement of the foreign domination of the Catholic Church in China. In Nanchang, the capital of Jiangxi province, the Jiangxi provincial government responded to American representations about the damage done to the missions with the claim that "no residence of the foreign missionaries has been burned." Monsignor O'Shea termed the statement "a shrewd evasion of the question at issue." O'Shea emphatically declared: "The property known as the Catholic mission in the section of South Kiangsi [Jiangxi] called Kannan, is all foreign property. Every mou [Chinese acre, equal to about a sixth of an English acre] of land has been bought with foreign money; every residence, church, chapel, school, or building of whatever kind, has been built with foreign money." And O'Shea had property deeds to back his claim. He further argued that the mission properties were still maintained by foreign money and that he, a foreigner, appointed Chinese or foreigners to occupy those properties as he saw fit. "It is only per accidens that native clergymen happened to be conducting those missions at the time they were burned. They are, and will remain, foreign property until such time as we judge expedient to entrust them to the native clergy."[8]

As events continued to demonstrate the weakness of the foreigners, the Vincentians experienced such an erosion of prestige that they feared for their control over Chinese Catholics. Some of them hoped that their government would take steps to restore their old prestige. No longer were the Vincentians able to protect their stations when manned by Chinese priests; Nationalist troops seized them for billets. Their followers looked to them for the exercise of a power which the Vincentians no longer had. The Christians in Anyuan, for example, were clamoring for reparations from the Nanjing government for the church which the Communists had burnt. In their opinion the Church as well as they had lost face. As Joseph Gately reported, "The pagans are jibbling about the powerlessness of the foreigners. A chink loves power." Gately felt that unless reparations were secured from the government, the lives and property of the missioners would "not mean a thing to the Chinese." Moreover, Gately was concerned that the spirit of nationalism current among Chinese Catholic seminarians would make it hard for foreigners to discipline them.[9]

The American consul general at Wuhan, F.P. Lockhart, was also quite interested in the matter of indemnification. Lockhart counted 112 cases in the years 1926-28 in which Chinese soldiers had taken over and destroyed American missionary property. He accounted it regrettable that few missionary societies had presented claims seeking indemnification for the losses sustained. Lockhart pointed out to Secretary of State Henry Stimson that practically every such case of occupation and deliberate destruction had been perpetrated "by armed forces belonging to organized Chinese armies and in recent months by troops of the Government recognized by the government of the United States."[10]

The Divergence of Vatican and United States Policy

Neither Gately nor Lockhart found officials of the Catholic Church eager to press claims for indemnification. Vatican policy was moving in another direction. That fact carried greater weight with O'Shea and other mission superiors than whatever they might hear from Washington's representatives. Similarly, it was the Vatican's policy to urge the missionaries to remain at their posts in times of danger rather than obey their consuls' orders to flee.

During the following winter, the divergence between State Department and Catholic missionary interests became clearer. After months of suspense, the Vincentians in Ganzhou finally faced the arrival of General Peng Dehuai's Communist forces in late January 1930. Monsignor O'Shea telegraphed the American consul general at Wuhan on behalf of the local general, begging him to urge Nanjing to send reinforcements immediately. The consul general advised O'Shea to leave Ganzhou. The American legation in Beijing also opposed the continued presence of Americans in the threatened area, but the bishop refused to leave.[11]

O'Shea's refusal to leave Ganzhou was based on mixed motives. He was reluctant to let steadfast European missionaries seem to be braver men and better missionaries than the Americans and he wanted to prove to Europeans that Americans could and would make good missioners. "Incidentally, in doing so," he wrote, "we prove that we are not a race of dollar chasers merely, but have a zealous faith that will equal if not overmatch the faith that Europeans have always manifested."[12] This statement of course clearly echoes the anxiety felt by James A. Walsh and other American Catholics over their lack of wholehearted acceptance by European Catholics as true Roman Catholics.

The bishop was also convinced that the continued American presence and presentation of facts through the American consuls had saved many lives and much property in the Ganzhou area. O'Shea claimed the right under treaty to remain in Ganzhou and lamented the sudden refusal of the American legation to represent his interests to the Chinese government. He also pointed out that the Nanjing government had asserted that it would protect foreign missionaries. To O'Shea, the new American policy seemed prompted only by the motive of avoiding the trouble which such representation entailed. He saw it as a betrayal of American interests.[13] Possibly he felt it as a denial of his claim to full citizenship and all its local privileges. Only by staying could he force his government to render him what he felt was his due as a citizen. In the crucible of besieged Ganzhou O'Shea would represent himself as truly Roman Catholic and fully an American citizen.

The armies of Zhu De and Peng Dehuai closed in on Ganzhou. A week before they began a seige which lasted from 15 March to 21 March 1930, the Ganzhou Chamber of Commerce begged O'Shea to telegram the U.S. consul to use his influence to keep the Nationalist 35th Brigade in town. Mindful of the U.S. legation's prior telegraphed refusal to ask for troops to protect Ganzhou missionaries, O'Shea declined. Finally, he did telegraph the Minister of Foreign Affairs, who promised soldiers and advised him to stay in Ganzhou.[14] Returning Nationalist forces defeated the Communists just as the city was about to fall.

The Communists extensively damaged the operations of the vicariate apostolic. They looted several stations near Ganzhou, including the Dawoli mission's huge convent, described by one Vincentian priest as a "palace."[15] The Sisters fled to Ganzhou. Several of the priests also fled from their stations; some of them went to Guangdong province for refuge.

When the Communist forces departed from the vicinity, they left behind propagandists whose work was so effective that the missioners could not safely go beyond the walls of Ganzhou. Indeed, only the presence of large numbers of Nationalist troops in the city made it possible for the missionaries to remain there.[16] When part of the soldiery left Ganzhou around the first of August, Bishop Dumond, the Sisters, and some of the priests left with them. The Sisters subsequently returned to America for several years.

In the two years that followed the siege of January 1930, mission work in the Ganzhou vicariate apostolic was minimal. The priests who had left the mission stayed away. Those who remained were overworked. Gains in the Tangjiang mission district and a record 1000 baptisms in the Dawoli mission district did not shake Monsignor O'Shea's pessimism about the vicariate's chances in the face of entrenched Communist opposition. He was convinced that the Nationalists' extermination campaigns would fail to eradicate the Jiangxi Soviet and also that there was no fundamental military solution to the problem of Communism. Yet by the autumn of 1931 the Ganzhou Vincentians were so overworked that O'Shea, in complete control of the vicariate after the assignment of Monsignor Dumond to be vicar apostolic of Nanchang, decided to take the risk of recalling his refugee missionaries from Guangdong and the United States. Otherwise, the mission effort might have collapsed altogether.[17]

The Communists wanted to capture Ganzhou as badly as O'Shea wanted to convert it. Soon after O'Shea recalled his men, the Communists began to move in on that key city. Tens of thousands of refugees fled from the surrounding territory and took refuge behind the city walls. The Vincentians fed and lodged 1000 of them; a heavy strain on mission finances resulted.[18] But the nervous strain was greater as the people of the city braced for the inevitable attack, taking what comfort they could from the presence of a few thousand Cantonese troops and, later, of 2000 Guangxi troops. The bulk of Nationalist forces were tied up by Japanese attacks in Manchuria and Shanghai. It seemed as if Ganzhou, a strategic town and a symbol of the urban-based Nationalists' resistance to the peasant warriors of the Jiangxi Soviet, would surely fall.

On February 4, 1932, tens of thousands of Communist troops besieged Ganzhou. The local Chamber of Commerce prompted O'Shea to telegraph the American consul for protection; the consul then called on Xiong Shi-hui, chairman of the Jiangxi provisional government. In Nanjing, the American consul general, Willys R. Peck, upon instruction of the American legation, made representations to the Ministry of Foreign Affairs. The Minister to China, Nelson T. Johnson, wrote to the Minister of Foreign Affairs on behalf of O'Shea.[19]

The siege dragged on for more than a month. The besiegers blew in all three of the city gates and kept tremendous pressure on the two regiments defending Ganzhou. In bitter fighting, the defenders exacted heavy losses from the Communists. Three shells landed on the mission and others hit the

Sisters' house, which held about 500 refugees. Fortunately, no one was hurt. At last, bowing to American pressure, the Nationalist government rushed three divisions of troops to the scene and raised the siege on March 7.

As a result of the military operations of early 1932, the Ganzhou vicariate apostolic sustained extensive material losses but surprisingly few apostasies. The Ganzhou mission compound itself sustained little damage; nearby mission stations were wrecked. If the missionaries had any consolation, it was that very few Catholics converted to Communism. The Catholics had told the Communists that they would do so after the fall of Ganzhoua and the confident revolutionaries had not bothered them. The missionaries thus found that their most pressing task was the care of the hundreds of refugees who crowded the Ganzhou mission compound for the next year. As late as January 1933, there were 1900 refugees there, most of them women.[20]

Communists and Nationalists as Enemies

To the north in the Yujiang vicariate apostolic, the American Vincentians suffered during the years 1926-1933 from occupation and pillage by Communist, provincial, and Nationalist troops, and by armed deserters. All but two of the Americans, Edward Sheehan and Leo Moore, abandoned the mission.

The Communists struck at the Church's status as an important landlord by seizing deeds and mortgages held by the missions. In 1928, for example, they carried off more than thirty mortgage deeds and ten property deeds belonging to the Catholic mission in Jingdezhen. Dozens of other deeds taken on that occasion either belonged to the mission or had been entrusted to it for safekeeping. A State Department official reacted to this news with the comment that "the American Catholics are emulating their French brethren in the matter of acquiring property both by mortgage and otherwise." He wished to ascertain how general that practice was among the American Catholic missions but his colleagues felt that the matter was too sensitive to bring up in the absence of official Chinese protests.[21]

The American head of the Yujiang vicariate apostolic was as bitter against the Nationalists as he was against the Communists. At his request, American diplomatic officials made representations to the Chinese government concerning damage to the missions. The representations were of little avail and Edward T. Sheehan, C.M., who assumed leadership of the vicariate apostolic in July 1929, became openly critical of the Nationalist government. Complaining to the American consul, Lockhart, on September 8, 1930, of the continuing occupation of the Yujiang mission compound by Nationalist troops, Sheehan telegraphed, "Nanking Government lies, lies, lies, lies. Demand action. My residence worth $1,000 a day. Occupied since May. If you demand payment these yellow rats will get out." Sheehan further complained to Lockhart on January 14, 1931, that the Nationalist government was doing everything possible in the interior, at least in Jiangxi province, to make life unbearable for foreigners.[22]

The Dominicans' Jian'ou mission also suffered as a result of the civil war. The passage of Communist forces through Jian'ou in 1928 sent the missioners fleeing and resulted in damage to the mission. In September 1930, armed soldiers took over the mission at Jienyang but left before June 1931. In May 1931, Fr. B.C. Werner reported that well-equipped Communist forces from Jiangxi were assisting local soviet forces in harassing the Chong'an district. The combined Communist forces defeated government troops and in the following month local Communists sacked Chong'an, destroyed the mission there, and burnt some homes of the wealthy. By year's end the missionaries recovered all of their property except the houses in Songxi and Nanhua and some land and building materials in Jian'ou. But the number of Dominicans had fallen to six, half as many as in 1926, and they were operating only four stations, eight fewer than in 1926. They estimated their monetary losses during that six-year period at $35,000. The Communists maintained their pressure on the Dominicans and in July and August 1932, the visiting American Dominican provincial superior, T.S. McDermott, found "far from encouraging conditions" in the mission territory.[23]

The Impact of Civil Disorder on the Other Missions

In Hunan, the Passionist Fathers returned from the safety of Guizhou province in late 1927 to find that their territory was far from safe or peaceful. Due to the widespread revolutionary fervor it was impossible in most places to open schools or other institutional works. Thus most of the priests worked alone trying to reclaim individual Christians who had drifted away from the Church. The threatened priests attended to their daily rounds of parochial duties: saying Mass, training altar boys, visiting the sick, and supervising schools where they could be opened. But death threw a cruel twist into their routines. On April 26, 1929, Fr. Constantine Leech died of typhoid fever at Yongshun. Only two days before bandits had murdered Frs. Godfrey Holbein of Baltimore, Maryland, Clement Seybold of Dunkirk, New York, and Walter Coveyou of Petoskey, Michigan. The bandits had taken the priests captive on their way from Chenxi to Zhijiang.[24]

The murders created a sensation in the ranks of the missionaries and their supporters. The State Department lodged a protest with the Chinese government. The Passionist provincial superior, however, was reluctant to press the issue in Washington. He saw little that the Chinese government could do in the isolated fastnesses of Hunan and he feared that if pushed on the matter the State Department would order all Americans from the area.[25]

More trials lay ahead of the Passionists and their co-workers. On April 19,

1932, the Charity Sisters' newly repaired convent in Yuanling burned down and in July one of their number, Sister Devota Ross of Brooklyn, New York, died of cholera in Chenxi. She had spent her energies nursing victims of a deadly cholera epidemic and also Fr. Raphael Vance, critically ill with dysentery and typhoid fever.[26]

The American Franciscans' Wuchang territory was another mission operation severely compromised by communist activities. Communist opposition prevented the Franciscans from even entering three of the six counties assigned to them. In the Xianning area there had been no resident priest since 1926. The school there had to be closed frequently because of molestation and occupation by the military. Even with these areas closed off, however, the Franciscans did not have enough priests to man the principal mission stations.[27]

The poor health of the Franciscan priests in the Wuchang territory posed still another problem for the mission. After visiting the area in late 1931, the provincial superior of the Franciscans' Cincinnati province, Fr. Freundt, was concerned for the physical well-being of the missionaries. He appealed to the members of his province to raise money to acquire a summer "resort" in cool mountains by the north China seaside. Then he wrote optimistically about the future of the mission. Buddhism, Daoism, and, most recently, Protestantism were failing. "Doubtless," he wrote, "the poverty and simplicity of the Order with its characteristic charity to the poor must have a special appeal to the minds of the Chinese, most of whom are attracted by the Franciscan principles of a true Christian life."[28]

The very size of the medical and educational works conducted by the Franciscan priests and the Sisters who worked with them may indeed have persuaded many local Chinese of the Americans' spirit of charity but it probably also confirmed them in their belief that the foreigners were anything but poor and simple. In addition to the hospital and dispensary work which constituted the greatest drain of the mission's resources, the vicariate apostolic of Wuchang in 1931 was operating sixty-two schools and fifty-six mission stations.

The bulk of the mission's medical and educational work was on the shoulders of the Catholic Sisters and their Chinese assistants. In Huanshi, the Sisters of Saint Francis from Luxemburg ran a hospital, a catechumenate, a school, dispensaries, and an orphanage. The Sisters of Charity from Mount Saint Joseph, Ohio, supported and conducted a hospital, a dispensary, an orphan asylum, and two homes for the aged in Wuchang. In Wuchang, the Sisters of Notre Dame de Namur from Reading, Ohio, supported and conducted a girls' middle school, which in the post-1928 period was seriously handicapped by uncooperative Chinese school officials. Also in Wuchang, the Franciscan Sisters from La Crosse, Wisconsin, funded and operated a parish school, a catechumenate for old women, and a dispensary. By July

1933, they had treated more than 188,000 patients free or at token cost. As of 1935 their school was self-supporting and the Sisters were cooperating with local leaders of China's New Life movement, who used the school on Sunday mornings to teach rudimentary reading to the illiterate. This progress was made despite division in the La Crosse Sisters' Wuchang community and the poor health of some of the Sisters.[29]

The pressure from the Communists which kept the Wuchang Franciscans from entering half of their mission territory also disrupted the promising work of the Sisters of Loretto across the Chang Jiang in Hanyang. The Sisters' school there had grown gradually until in 1930 there were 117 female students. But in August 1930, disaster struck. First, the approach of Communist forces caused the Sisters to send home those country girls who would go. Then, on the eleventh of August, they fled to the safety of Wuhan with sixty-five pupils. Next, severe flooding put two-thirds of the Hanyang vicariate under water and the Sisters turned from education to relief work. They housed and fed 250 refugees in the school and offered those interested a catechism course. In the following August, the flooding occurred once more and the Communists remained a disruptive threat until they were driven from the area in 1932.

The Sisters became so confident of their ability to cope with the situation in Hanyang that when asked in 1933 to begin an English-medium combined elementary and high school for girls in Shanghai, they accepted. The arrival of four more Sisters from America made it possible to open Loretto School, as it was called, in September 1933. Operating on an eight-year elementary and four-year secondary school system, the school was registered with the Chinese government as a private foreign school.[30]

One hundred miles upriver from Wuchang and Hanyang, American Franciscans from the New York province were just beginning work in a five-county area around the city of Shashi. The New York Franciscans had spurned the counsel of Franciscan authorities in Rome that they work in the Zibo, Shandong, mission with the friars from the St. Louis province. Instead, they had decided to work in Shaanxi province. After those plans collapsed, the few New York province missionaries worked in a four-county area around Shaoyang in central Hunan from late 1929 until 1932. Then they took up an invitation to work in the vicariate apostolic of Yichang, Hubei. Their new independent mission stretched over low-lying ground on both sides of the Chang Jiang. The first two American Franciscans on the scene found that all the mission stations in the area had been totally or partially destroyed by Communists in the preceding years. The morale of the Catholic community was low.[31]

Conditions in the Kaifeng, Henan, area were similarly difficult for the missionaries. Until April 1929, it was not safe for the Providence Sisters to return to that important city. Once back in Kaifeng, the Sisters began the delicate task of establishing a native sisterhood, the Providence Sisters Catechists. While they were initiating the Sisters Catechists, they were also trying to reestablish older works. Unable to comply with the Nationalist government's new educational regulations, they poured their extra energies into orphanage work. Sr. Gratia Luking continued to guide the Sisters Catechists, encouraging them to learn the rudiments of pharmacology and nursing as other means of reaching the people.[32]

Years passed before the Sisters could reinstitute formal educational activity and even then they experienced difficulty. In the autumn of 1932, despite widespread antiforeign feeling, the Sisters were able to purchase a large property as the site of a junior middle and upper middle school for girls. They named the enterprise Jing Yi School. In compliance with government regulations, the principal of the school and the nine members of its board of directors were Chinese. Furthermore, no religion was taught on the school premises; the Sisters gave religious instruction at their house on Sundays. The Board of Education awarded the school an "A" rating but required more dormitory space. The Sisters managed to add a three-story dormitory by fall 1933.[33]

Conditions in the Zibo, Shandong, mission of the Franciscans were much less promising. Work in that territory had advanced slowly through the initial years of the depression and in 1932 mission operations had to be cut back.[34] It would take the arrival of several groups of Sisters to restore some dynamism to the mission.

The Depression Strikes Fu Ren University

The history of Fu Ren University during these years was one of progress after setbacks. In July 1927, the Beijing government Ministry of Education officially recognized Fu Ren as a university. In June 1929, however, the Ministry of Education at Nanjing demoted Fu Ren to the rank of college. Under the regulations of the Nanjing government, only institutions with faculties of arts and sciences and at least one additional faculty were entitled to the rank of university. As a result of the government's action, Fu Ren officials moved quickly to institute a faculty of sciences with appropriate building and equipment. The Nanjing government consequently restored Fu Jen to university status in August 1929.

Fu Jen administrators planned further expansion. Fr. Francis Clougherty, O.S.B., succeeded the recently deceased Rev. Aurelius Stehle, O.S.B., as chancellor of Fu Jen in August 1930. The Benedictines assigned two more confreres to the university as science teachers and Clougherty recruited a contingent of Benedictine Sisters from St. Benedict's College, St. Joseph, Minnesota, to found a woman's college at the university.[35]

Economic stringency foreclosed any chance of developing a woman's college at Fu Ren. When the Benedictine Sisters arrived in September 1930, they quickly discovered that they did not have the resources at hand to undertake such a work. So, as they studied Chinese, they laid plans for a girls' senior high school. The Benedictine Sisters remained at Fu Ren only until the graduation of their first class in 1935. The Sister Servants of the Holy Ghost, a female organization parallel to the Society of the Divine Word and having the same founder, replaced them. The Benedictines went to Kaifeng where two of them, Ronayne Gergen and Wibora Muehlenbein, taught in the English department of Henan University and the other six or seven opened a dispensary and did some educational work.[36]

For economic reasons the Benedictine priests also lost their place at Fu Ren. As the depression deepened, both the ability of the Benedictine Fathers to support the university and the prospects for the institution's existence shriveled. In January 1932, Fu Ren's rector, George Barry O'Toole, left Beijing on a fundraising tour of the United States. Well aware of the financial dangers, officials of Propaganda Fide informed O'Toole as he was passing through Rome in February 1933 that they were considering asking the Society of the Divine Word to take over Fu Ren.[37] Negotiations to that end began in Beijing in late May and on June 20, 1933, care of the university was transferred to the Society of the Divine Word. An American, Fr. Joseph P. Murphy, was appointed Rector of the university and superior of the Divine Word community there on July 4, 1933. On August 5, 1933, V. Rev. Joseph Grendel, superior general of the society, succeeded Francis Clougherty as chancellor.

Propaganda Fide's move was very timely, for the Benedictine Archabbey which had provided the building money for Fu Ren subsequently became insolvent. By that time Fu Ren was beyond the reach of the Archabbey's creditors.[38] Those Benedictine priests who wished to remain in China, Francis Clougherty among them, went to Kaifeng where they took up educational work.[39]

The Economic Difficulties of the Fushun Mission

To the north in Manchuria, Maryknoll missionaries were experiencing not only financial problems but also difficult pastoral challenges and the dangers of war. The financial problems were never completely solved. The Americans had taken over a 32,000-square-mile portion of the Shenyang (Mukden) vicariate apostolic from the Paris Foreign Mission Society. From the beginning of the Maryknoll effort, the French refused to contribute to the support of the Americans or their work. They had the funds to do so, millions in Boxer indemnity money.[40] Instead, they demanded that the Americans support the handful of Chinese priests working in the territory and reimburse the French mission for the run-down property turned over to the Maryknollers. The Americans believed that the French were deliberately trying to exploit them financially—that the Americans had "all of the 'onus' but none of the 'bonus.' "[41]

Upkeep and operation of the farflung territory was expensive. The Fushun mission boundaries encompassed both rural areas and bustling cities, including Fushun, Dandong, Linjiang, and Xinbin. In addition to the central residence in Fushun, there were six chapels with residences and fifteen chapels without residences. Each of the mission's districts had catechism schools and prayer schools in which both secular and religious subjects were taught. There were also orphanages and catechumenates. The 3000 to 3500 Catholics in the territory were very poor and could provide little financial support for such a large enterprise. Furthermore, the properties owned by the mission did not produce enough revenue to keep the old mission buildings in repair, let alone pay for the priests' educational work.[42]

By mid-1930 the Fushun mission had reached a financial crisis. There was no money to make needed major repairs to its old buildings or to build schools and chapels. Alms from the United States were uncertain at best and the mission's thirty or forty housing units were costing more to keep up than the $150 they annually produced in rent. In effect, the hard-pressed mission was subsidizing its tenants, most of them Catholics. A gift of $4700 from Propaganda Fide for the fiscal year 1930-31 was not sufficient to ease the situation.[43]

The local Maryknoll superior, J.P. McCormack, went to Beijing to see the apostolic delegate about the financial condition of his mission territory and about its impending separation from the Shenyang vicariate apostolic. The delegate's secretary, Fr. Antonutti, met the worried McCormack with a smile, a promise of $10,000 a year, and word that St. Peter's Work Society, a European organization specializing in the support of seminaries in foreign lands, would provide the money for a new preparatory seminary and for scholarship funds. Then he told McCormack that the proposed Fushun vicariate apostolic would receive nothing of the Shenyang vicariate apostolic's treasure. Citing Canon 1500, Antonutti explained that since America promised to be a richer source of alms than France did, the Americans had no claim on a share of the Paris Foreign Mission Society's investments. Since the Maryknoll missions in South China had gotten along well without help from the original missions, the Italian felt that the proposed Maryknoll Fushun mission would do well too. McCormack was bitter.[44]

During the summer of the following year, 1931, the American priests and the vicar apostolic of Shenyang worked out the details of a settlement separating the Maryknoll mission from the vicariate apostolic of Shenyang. The change became effective in 1932, but financial problems continued to dog the newly independent Maryknoll mission, hampering institutional work. To keep down food and fuel bills, for example, the Maryknoll priests in Fushun sent their preparatory seminarians home for two months at Chinese New Year. They also devoted much thought to the development of an income-producing wood working department. Nonetheless, throughout the depression, the priests at the central mission stations were well cared for by the Maryknoll Society. One missionary writing from Linjiang to a stateside confrere wondered "where the hardships of the mission come in." He considered himself and his fellow missionaries "pretty lucky 'birds' to be on the other side of the water, while you all at home have the real problems to contend with."[45]

While the Americans were trying to cope with the financial limitations on their enterprise, they also struggled to manage a complex pastoral situation among the Chinese, Korean, Japanese, Irish, English, Portuguese, French, and American Roman Catholics in Dandong. To instruct and preach to the Koreans, the Maryknollers each Thursday brought in a Korean catechist from across the Yalu River. A Korean priest came over once a month to say Mass for his compatriots. For the Chinese boys and girls there was a very small catechetical school; many of the Chinese, however, lacked instruction and the American priests were slow in remedying that. The lack of fervor of the occidental Catholics was an embarrassment to the priests, as it was to missionaries elsewhere in China. And in the shadowy background there was always the competition of well-financed Protestant missionaries with their schools and orphanages.[46]

The Impact of Japanese Aggression

Even as the American Catholic priests were removing their operation from French ecclesiastical control and struggling to resolve their financial and pastoral problems, an era of personal danger and Japanese restrictions was at hand. Until June 1931, the turbulence of Manchurian life passed the Maryknollers by. Then, on June 22, bandits held up a missioner in Fushun and released him unharmed. From the night of September 18-19, the date of the "Mukden [Shenyang] Incident" and the beginnings of the swift advance of Japan's Guandong Army across Manchuria, the Maryknollers experienced much greater danger than before.

Although both Japanese and Chinese officials were solicitous of the safety of the American missionaries, the priests maintained they were in little danger from bandits and would take no sides in the military conflict, leaving politics to the politicians. Yet in the Donghua area, members of the Big Sword Society and the disbanded Chinese soldiers who made up the local resistance to the puppet government of Manzuguo (proclaimed by the Japanese in March 1932) had no doubts as to whose side the Americans were on. The Maryknollers freely passed through their roadside ambush points as they traveled around the Tonghua-Erbashi mission district. The Big Swords escorted all Japanese from the contested area and proclaimed themselves all friends with Americans.[47]

Summer came and the fighting continued. Linjiang lay in almost total ruin that July after fighting broke out on the eleventh of the month. The little Catholic hospital there survived and provided care for the wounded.[48] In Xinbin there was also great danger and suffering. The two Maryknoll priests there who attended to the wounded were very careful to avoid offending military authorities. Their prudence was well advised, for the temper of the soldiery was volatile, as Fr. Thomas Quirk learned in the Erbashi district. The disbanded Chinese soldiers harassed him and the Big Swords forbade Catholics to visit him in the church compound at Tongshanzi, so Quirk withdrew to the dubious safety of Fushun.

That summer and fall the mission compounds were dangerous. The Japanese dropped several fifty-two-pound bombs in and about the compound at Erbashi and killed one Christian. A dud landed in front of the priest's house. The Maryknollers made no claims for repairs and merely called on the Japanese authorities to prevent further damage. The priests also attempted, unsuccessfully, to hush up the incident at Fushun in which Maryknollers and those to whom they had given asylum were caught under Japanese bombs. Ten Christians were killed. The mission superior, Raymond A. Lane, back at his post after a three-year term on the Maryknoll Society's General Council, refused to talk with newspapermen about the incident and advised the only Chinese survivor, an old woman, not to talk. He also refused to give the American consul any information because to have done so would have caused the priests embarrassment. Lane, who knew that the Japanese were opening the Americans' mail and were highly suspicious of the Maryknollers' use of code in their communications, did not want to irritate the conquerors.[49]

Despite the caution of the American Catholics, the Japanese authorities were concerned that the missionaries would utilize their extensive mission establishment to gather and transmit information on Japanese operations in Manchuria.[50] Japanese suspicions soon surfaced in the Shenyang *Shengching Shibao*, the Shenyang *Hoten Mainichi,* and the Dalian *Xin Bao*. The newspapers all carried similar articles on November 21, 1933, stating what the Maryknoll personnel already knew to be true, that the Manzuguo and Japanese police forces were keeping a close eye on them. The article commented on the missioners' extensive contacts with the people and described the most recently arrived American Catholic missioners as "university graduates and much aware of economics, medicine, farming and engineering, besides theology." Because of the priests' numerous contacts with the people and opportunities to gather information which they could pass on to the American government, the writer called the Maryknollers "spies in disguise." The presence in the American mission of Chinese priests allegedly trained in the Americans' seminary made "the disposition of their forces complete" in the eyes of the Japanese dispatch writer. He completed his case with the allegation that American soldiers or officers in priestly cassocks were among the group of missioners.[51]

The Maryknollers reacted strongly. In company with the American vice-consul at Fushun, a Maryknoll representative called on the Japanese vice-consul at Fushun and complained about the article. The Japanese official was courteous and promised to seek a public retraction. The missionaries took further action; they published a well-received pamphlet explaining the work of the Catholic Church and its missions in Manzuguo. The attacks in the newspapers ceased; but the Japanese police continued a petty persecution of the priests that one Maryknoll missionary labeled "most infantile and puerile," making missionary work more difficult.[52]

Morale Problems

The fighting and depression made the American Catholic religious societies reluctant to commit additional personnel and support to the China missions. Fear of being sent to China chilled the missionary ardor of the members of several societies. Reinforcements of priests became sporadic and many stateside colleagues in America ceased corresponding with the missionaries, who were often isolated from one another. A sense of abandonment seized many of the missionaries. Some of them reacted by trying to enlist the most indoctrinated and disciplined of their communities, the seminarians. James Corbett, for example, promised Vincentian novices that foreign mission work was "forever presenting new problems and gives wide latitude of choice in the matter of plans." Very few of them turned to the China mission as an escape from what Corbett called the "determined, cut-and-dried, institutional or bound by traditions" home mission work.[53]

Where military activity did not threaten the lives of missionaries and provide them with a ready explanation for the slow development of their missions, missionaries felt keenly their lack of success. In the Pingnan area of the Wuzhou mission, progress was so slow through 1932 that a new China missionary, Fr. Buckley, questioned the concept of concentrating on the conversion of country people to the neglect of work among urban folk. Buckley's questioning had no effect on Maryknoll policy and the prospect of meager results deeply affected him. He had learned in the seminary that the missioner's greatest trials would not be physical but spiritual, the pain of disappointment in seeing hard work yield little or nothing. For that he had steeled himself. But he and others had discounted what he now believed to be a fact, "that the missioner who at the end of his life had meager results (from a rational point of view) is not the exception but very common."[54]

James E. Walsh, leader of the adjacent Jiangmen mission was concerned by its slight progress. During his initial period as a local Maryknoll superior, the needs of the society to expand its territory had governed his thinking and policies. His next preoccupation had been surviving Chinese hostility. The evaporation of trouble from local Communists and Nationalists and the ebbing of anti-Christian feeling during the spring of 1929 cleared away external excuses for the Jiangmen mission's lack of success. Walsh reached the conclusion "that the need of this work is not money but men. We are playing at real mission work simply because the few men in the understaffed missions of China are all absorbed in running their little organizations. There is almost nobody to do the real work of converting pagans." He thought it possible that churchmen would "have to enlist *armies* of men" to mount "an intelligent attack on paganism."[55]

A sense of futility continued to pervade the thinking of the Jiangmen mission leader. In his report to the Maryknoll Society's 1929 General Chapter (the representative governing body in session), Walsh pointed out that although the mission had done all the indispensable construction work, including four new mission stations opened in the previous month—an all-time high—there was still need for a central training school for catechists, of whom there was a "desperate" shortage. Time was running out, he reported. Within a few years "the march of materialism" would penetrate the countryside and blight the "laborious, simple, and unspoiled" peasantry, who, the bishop felt, were still "approachable and kindly and good, . . . promising subjects for the sweet yoke of Christ." The mission needed catechists to reach these people since a catechumenate consumed "too much rice for any but wealthy missions to contemplate." As it was, Walsh concluded, "Instead of making converts we almost fear to see them come, since we lack the machinery, viz., priests and catechists to care for them properly."[56]

The situation in the Jiangmen vicariate apostolic did not greatly change during 1930. Educational and parochial work as well as building went on. Sickness and death thinned the scanty ranks of the missioners and the isolation of those who remained was increased. In itself the isolation was significant for the future. Fr. Joseph McGinn wrote in the Chiqi (Chikkai) mission diary that as a result of living alone he had developed "peculiar traits" and it took him "quite a while to realize that there was another English-speaking man in the house." He felt that his fellow Maryknoller must have wondered about his sanity or at least his urbanity. "Alas!" he wrote, "I feel that I shall never again be a plastic subject for life in community. One does get 'queer!' " Thus customary solitude reinforced the prevailing individualism. McGinn shortly thereafter began building an orphan asylum and his mission school flourished as never before, having sixty students, mostly non-Christians.[57]

Such work did not impress the vicar apostolic of Jiangmen and he remained pessimistic. In 1931, he reported to J.A. Walsh that his vicariate apostolic had made no progress over the past five years because it had been "hopelessly crippled by our small recruitment of recent years. For a while we tried to advance in spite of it; latterly I have told the men not even to try. We are making almost no converts." The few missionaries were absorbed just with keeping the large vicariate going. The Jiangmen Maryknollers were still encountering antimission propaganda and finding among the people at large "a little less politeness perhaps, a little more ridicule at times, a slightly colder shoulder in general." And that summer in explaining the poor record of conversions made by his operation in 1930-31, the bishop summed up his view of the mission situation: "A few men with a few stammered words cannot convert hordes, yet such is practically our present effort." In 1933, the demoralized Walsh wrote, "Apart from doing what the Church ordains, no policy exists in missions. For the rest circumstance rules; although circumstance itself in turn is also ruled, of course, by a higher power. If a suspended mind is the sign of a philosopher missioners would pass for so many Aristotles. They came to China indeed to carry messages to Garcia, but they remain to await messages from Providence."[58]

6

Life at the Margin

The basic strategy of the Roman Catholic church in China was to attract socially marginal Chinese and to hold their allegiance through a strong network of institutions. Under the leadership of the French, Catholic missionaries gathered up hundreds of thousands of the most marginal of all Chinese, female foundlings, and raised them as Christians in scores of orphanages. The missionaries sought converts among non-Han and Han Chinese, by manipulating the Chinese court system on behalf of clients with little claim to a favorable judgment and by providing institutional care for the homeless aged and leprous.

Many of the American Catholic missionaries, not fully conscious of this marginality, failed to account for it in their assessment of church activities and prospects; others were more perceptive. Some of them saw opportunities in attracting the socially marginal; others saw a socially marginal membership as a problem for the Church, because it reinforced the church's status as a marginal institution.

The Strategic Problem Facing the Church

Few American Catholics could face the Roman Church's failure to draw people from the Chinese mainstream. Both American Catholic missionaries in China and their supporters in the United States interpreted the limited successes in China as harbingers of general success. Their misunderstanding of the missionary enterprise reduced consideration of the future of the China missions to a debate over tactics and operational policy.

The Maryknollers in South China noted that their three missions followed different policies and had different results. The most successful of the three Maryknoll missions in numbers of converts was the Mei Xian territory under Francis X. Ford. Ford allowed no mission dispensaries or asylums of any kind in his territory and downplayed the role of schools.[1] He stressed proselytization so strongly that he ordered the Maryknoll Sisters to leave their convents for weeks at a time to live together in pairs among the peasants of the countryside so that they might more easily reach the local people.[2] James E. Walsh in the Jiangmen mission stressed the role of charitable and educational institutions in attracting the Chinese. Under Bernard Meyer's leadership, the Wuzhou mission tried to strike a balance between proselytization and institutional endeavors by combining a vigorous catechetical program with numerous rudimentary and elementary schools and dispensaries. Ford's mission won the most converts; Meyer's almost as many; Walsh's by far the fewest. The missionaries attributed the relative success of Ford's mission to his emphasis on proselytization and the relative failure of Walsh's mission to his stress on institutions. They shaped their thinking on the future of their missions accordingly.

The relative success or failure of the missions was more closely tied to the number of marginal people in their audience than to their tactics. In fact, all three of the Maryknoll South China missions were oriented toward attracting outcasts and people marginal to Chinese society. Full consciousness of this, however, did not pervade the missionary community. Ford's mission in an isolated, mountainous area worked with the largest pool of marginal people, the Hakka, a group possessing a long and bloody history of strife with the main body of Han Chinese. For the Hakka, acceptance of Christianity only formalized in one more way their alienation from their fellow Han and provided them with a link to the foreign overlords of China. The somewhat less geographically isolated Wuzhou mission drew its converts from among the poor peasants. Town dwellers resisted the overtures of the missionaries and, as a result, after more than a decade of missionary activity, there were only ninety Christians in Wuzhou.[3] The Jiangmen mission was the least isolated and the most affected by the main currents of Han Chinese society. Its successes, when measured in terms of converts, were the fewest.

A contemporary Maryknoll official, John Considine, grasped the correlation of social marginality and receptivity to Christianity. From his office in Rome, Considine sought to console the first vicar apostolic of Jiangmen, who was disheartened by the sparsity of converts among the antiforeign Han Chinese. Considine assured his fellow American that the lack of conversions in Jiangmen was in line with the global Roman Catholic mission situation. Considine had visited mission areas around the world and was able to report that most progress in the mission work was coming "in little sectors, principally among aborigines, where the missioners scouring desperately the territory for which they are responsible stumble upon weak points in the defenses of Satan and push in for a little victory." The aborigines were "the backwash . . . forgotten both by men and the devil. Nevertheless," wrote Considine, "with such primitive material, the Church will build its empire."

He advised his confrere in Guangdong that, if there were such aborigines in his vicariate apostolic, then he should concentrate his liquid capital on those people; the ensuing gains would boost the morale of all his co-workers.[4]

A few of the American Catholic missionaries in China grasped the situation as well as Considine did. Charles Simons, an American Jesuit of the California Province, understood that if the Church were to make converts, those converts would have to come from among Chinese not caught up in China's modernization. While some of his fellow American Jesuits labored to establish an English-medium high school in Shanghai, Simons began work with French Jesuits in the countryside near Donghai, Jiangsu. Although some of the French obviously resented the coming of the American, Simons was more impressed by the relative absence of antiforeign sentiment among the desperately poor local Chinese. That condition would pass, he feared, with the opening of a seaport in the district. "Please God," he wrote, "missionaries can keep ahead of merchants and reap a good part of their harvest before an activized foreign commerce comes to blight it."[5]

One colleague who had altogether different plans for church work shared Simon's fear that events in China were working against the Roman Church. George Dunne saw no great future for the Church if it concentrated on the peasantry as Simons was urging. Nor did he support Gonzaga High School, the American Jesuits' project in Shanghai. Dunne told the Jesuit superior who had made the high school a pet project that he had no vocation to spend his life "puttering around Shanghai looking out after a handful of expatriated foreigners most of whom have no business here except that of making money off the Chinese."[6] Instead of tending to marginal people such as peasants or expatriate Westerners, Dunne wished to influence the leadership of China.

In a lengthy document which outlined his thinking on the bleak prospects of the Church in China, Dunne expressed alarm over the fact that the Church had virtually no influence among Chinese intellectuals. "Catholic higher education remains ridiculously insignificant," he wrote. At the same time, he found, "All the currents of thought in China are of the worst kind, inspired by materialistic, rationalistic, atheistic philosophies of the West. Such is the inspiration of government circles, educational circles, literary circles, intellectual circles in general. Immense outpouring of literature of the same inspiration. An Absolute State inspired by these ideas will be the *ruination of the Church in China*. China moving rapidly in that direction." Hastening the movement were more than thirty Chinese state universities largely staffed by returned students who had imbibed "all that is worst in Western culture," more than thirty Protestant mission universities spreading not Christian thought but "rationalistic protestant thought much more vicious in its consequences than simple paganism," and a great number of "private (pagan) universities."[7]

Dunne convinced Church authorities in Rome and China that just as Matteo Ricci and his successors at the imperial court had made it possible for Catholicism to spread in China, so a small group of highly educated missionaries working in Nanjing would be able to establish Church prestige and spread Catholic thought. Dunne's plan called for a few highly capable specialists drawn from all the American Jesuit provinces. They would work in collaboration with the Chinese government on "educational, sociological, economic, and agricultural problems." They would establish a small institute in Nanjing and tutor Chinese students. They would "employ every means their ingenuity and talent can devise to spread Catholic ideas, influence thought, [and] gain prestige."[8]

Dunne's plan did not reach fruition. The other American Jesuit provinces were slow to cooperate in the new project and nothing more than the foundation of the institute's physical plant had been completed when the Japanese sacked Nanjing. The American Jesuits in Nanjing and Shanghai then gave their energies to relief work.[9] When the immediate crisis passed, most of the Jesuits returned to high school or parish work in Shanghai or to lengthy theological studies and so were unable to initiate or sustain any significant work in China before the Japanese interned them at Xujiawei seminary after the attack on Pearl Harbor.

Other missionaries feared that the Church's marginal membership threatened its future. While Dunne concerned himself with the external threat to the Church posed by intellectually hostile elites, the Maryknoller T.V. Kiernan worried that the illiterate peasants who were entering the Church would not be able to provide the cadres necessary to the Church's survival. "Is the Church in mission lands to be everlastingly composed of illiterates? Not until the Church has produced a goodly number of intelligent, educated and pious Catholics," he wrote, "can we hope for that condition which is called an 'indigenous Church.' "[10] Kiernan longed for funds to conduct a large scale educational program to school his illiterate followers in the Pingnan district of the Wuzhou mission. He hoped thereby to attract to the Church a higher class of Chinese.

The Continued Deterioration of the Church's Position

The Church lacked the funds to operate an institutional network which could better educate and indoctrinate the Chinese laity and attract non-Christians. The depression restricted donations from the United States just when additional money was needed to replace facilities destroyed by Nationalists and Communists. Operation of existing facilities became economically burdensome; replacement of facilities was extremely difficult. Under the pressure, the Church began to cut back its operations in some areas and to contemplate cutbacks in others. The patterns of mission work unraveled, Chinese Catholics drifted away from the Church, and some of the missionaries became demoralized.

During 1933, widespread Communist military and propaganda operations closed all but four of the mission stations in the American Vincentians' Ganzhou territory. The priests lost contact with two-thirds of their followers and with one another. As of February 1934, Fr. Francis Flaherty, stationed in Longnan, hadn't seen a confrere in two years or the vicar apostolic in four years. Despite the cutbacks in mission work, expenses continued at the previous year's level of $120,000.[11]

Some newly arrived missionaries were shocked to find that the Chinese Catholics whom the Vincentians could reach were often barely indoctrinated members whose behavior disappointed the clergy. The Vincentians did not publicize this fact in their popular accounts of mission work. They wrote of the good Christians and of the physical danger and hardship, not of "the large percentage of opium smokers, gamblers, and other lax Christians" whom Fr. Frederick McGuire found in his territory. He wanted to tell American Catholics the whole truth about the Church in China. During a heated argument, a colleague asked him, "Why spread all the dirt about the large number of bad christians?" "It is true," wrote McGuire's indignant fellow missioner, "that we have them and that they cause us the greatest difficulties, greater indefinitely than all the physical harships which we have to endure." He argued that the missionaries had to protect the good name of the seventy-five percent who were good Christians and he urged complete censorship of all articles by McGuire and other recently arrived missionaries.[12]

The Ganzhou mission Vincentians and the Chinese priests who worked under them slowly regained contact with their followers. In 1936 about forty-one percent of the nominal membership received Communion during the Eastertime. The priests found, however, that in their absence the mission's cathechetical system and rudimentary school network had failed to indoctrinate large numbers of Christians. In Tangjiang, Fr. John Munday discovered that he had more than 1000 Christians who knew almost nothing of Christianity despite the work of forty teachers in thirty mission-operated schools.[13]

External political and economic factors contributed to the continuing disintegration of the Ganzhou mission. In the Xinfeng area during the summer of 1935, roving bands of Communists kept the priests in their central stations at night and prevented visitation of distant outstations. Disruption was worse around Ningdu. Monsignor O'Shea visited the area in November 1935, and announced that the Church there was a temporal and moral ruins. He foresaw years of "hard sledding" for the Church there.[14]

The sledding was to be even harder for the Ganzhou mission than the bishop realized, for the economic depression would continue to diminish the work of his mission and the morale of the missionaries. To Fr. Larry Curtis in Dawoli, the shortage of money meant that he had to close down all outside schools and cut back on personnel. He feared that all progress made by him in seven years at Dawoli would be lost. Eighteen months later, in June 1937, Curtis reported that his fears were coming true. Fewer and fewer people were appearing at the catechumenate for instruction either because the bishop lacked money to provide free food for the cathechumens or because of the priests' lack of zeal. In the gloom that pervaded the Ganzhou mission during these years there was one bright spot, the effective work of the Sisters at the Ganzhou mission hospital.[15]

Troubled political and military conditions were also crippling the work of the Dominicans' Jian'ou, Fujian, mission. Communists and Nationalists both took their toll. From June 1933, the Soviet government of North Fujian held the mission property in Chong'an. On two occasions Communist forces occupied the station in San Gang in the southwestern part of Chong'an district and, on at least four occasions, the Huanggeng property in the northwestern part of Jianyang district. The Nationalists, however, had a worse impact on the mission. In October 1933, Nationalist troops took over the Jianyang mission station. In early December, another Nationalist military unit occupied the same mission compound. It was the twentieth time by the Dominicans' reckoning that Nationalist troops had forcibly occupied the Jianyang mission. The Jian'ou station, occupied only four times in the same period, was relatively peaceful.[16]

The Dominicans' status as United States nationals did not offer them much protection. In February 1934, the American minister at Beijing protested to the Nanjing government the forcible occupation of the Dominican missions in Jian'ou and Jianyang. Yet as of early April, the Public Road Construction Bureau still occupied the Jianyang mission. In May 1934, the government telegraph office took over the mission at Songxi.[17]

By 1935 the condition of the Jian'ou mission was precarious. Communist activity and frequent military operations made mission work dangerous and often impossible. Clusters of Christians had been totally devastated and scattered. The support of the refugees who came to the Dominicans for relief was an extremely onerous burden. Despite their relief efforts, the Dominicans lost at least a quarter of their following.[18]

The Dominican missionaries in Jian'ou also suffered losses of a personal nature. The Dominican sisterhood based in Columbus, Ohio, had taken a dozen years to carry out its less-than-whole hearted decision to send Sisters to troubled Fujian. Two of the five Dominican Sisters who began work in Jian'ou in mid-March 1936 died within fifteen months of their arrival. Sister M. Hildegarde Sapp, O.P., sixty-three years of age, a native of Danville, Ohio, died, probably of cancer, on December 27, 1936. Less than six months later, in June 1937, the thirty-three-year-old Sr. M. Leocadia Moore, O.P., a native of Pittsburgh, Pennsylvania, died. The editors of the Dominicans' mission magazine, *The Torch,* printed the news of her death in the back pages of their September issue.[19]

The state of the Passionists' northwestern Hunan mission was even more grim than that of the Dominicans' Fujian mission. Because of the proximity of the Communist Second Front Army, both 1934 and 1935 were years of great strain and worry for the missionaries. When the Communist troops finally moved into the territory in the spring of 1935, they singled out the missionaries for attack and drove Fr. Bonaventure Griffiths from his Yungshun station to Yuanling. The Communists then put so much pressure on Yuanling that Griffiths shepherded the mission's fifteen Sisters to Wuhan while Monsignor O'Gara and many of the priests fled into the hills for safety.[20] As a result of the disruption, slightly over half of the territory's 3117 Catholics lost contact with the Church and disappeared among a population of 4,500,000.[21]

The Church also lost contact with a large portion of its membership in the Franciscans' Wuchang mission. Under the leadership of the dynamic friar, Sylvester Espelage, a group of Franciscan priests, several laymen and laywomen, four groups of foreign Sisters, and a group of Chinese Sisters labored to convert people from the mainstream of Chinese society through an extensive medical and educational system. In 1935-36 the mission schools served 2000; the seven dispensaries, 103,605 outpatients; the two hospitals, 1606 patients; three orphanages, 185 children. Despite this benevolent activity, thirty-five percent of the laity gave up the practices of Catholicism and there were fewer than ten adult converts for each mission worker. Failing to hold the allegiance of thirty-five percent of their followers and unable to convert impressive numbers of Chinese, the Franciscans sought success at the ultimate margin of society: they hovered over the beds of the moribund and in 1935-36 baptized 3896 infants and 544 adults who were dying.[22]

Further up the Chang Jiang in Hubei province, another American Franciscan mission was conducting a vigorous outreach program. By 1936, when the Vatican raised the Shashi mission to the rank of prefecture apostolic, there were ten priests, two Brothers, and five Sisters working in the territory. They concentrated their efforts on dispensary aid and educational work. Three dispensaries in Shashi and many smaller ones in the countryside were under Franciscan operation. More than 800 boys studied in the mission's government-recognized schools. This was a vast change from 1932, when there had been only one mission school with fewer than twenty girl pupils.[23] Mission work in Shashi continued to gather momentum until the Second Sino-Japanese War broke out and refugees inundated the Franciscan stations.

Developments in the Zibo, Shandong, Franciscan mission demonstrated that extensive activity did not guarantee a flourishing mission. The arrival of

three groups of Sisters, the Sisters Adorers of the Precious Blood from Ruma, Illinois, the Sisters of St. Francis of Springfield, Illinois, and the Sisters of Saint Francis of Dubuque, Iowa, electrified a listless operation. The Sisters did extensive educational and dispensary work. By 1935-36 2700 pupils crowded the mission's many schools and 45,000 people visited its free clinics. Converts, entering the Church at a rate of thirty per missionary, were three times as numerous as in 1932. Yet a full third of the adult membership dropped their affiliation with the Church and forty-three percent of the Catholics who married that year married non-Christians.[24] The long-range prospects of the mission were not very good.

The Maryknoll mission in the Fushun, Manchuria, territory was also experiencing serious difficulties, though of a different sort. Financial stringency compromised the Maryknoll program. Although the Maryknoll Society continued to give the Fushun mission a good deal of assistance, Propaganda Fide slashed its annual contribution to the mission by 28 percent from 1932 to 1934.[25] The priests chose to use their diminished resources to develop government-recognized school programs at Dandong, Shanchengzi, and Tonghua and to increase to forty-two the number of orphans in their care. Although they curtailed dispensary work, other serious problems compounded the financial difficulties. Official Japanese restrictions and the linguistic challenge posed by a mixed population of Orientals and Occidentals hampered church work.

The Maryknoll missioners in Manchuria were poor proselytizers. Although they succeeded in attracting almost half as many catechumens as there were Christians in their territory, they were much less successful in persuading the Chinese to enter the Church as members. A confidential Vatican document giving the ratio of converts to missionary priests in the missions of China placed the Fushun mission, with eleven converts per priest, fourth among the six missions of Manchuria. The Fushun convert-to-priest ratio was more than twice as high as the Jiangmen mission (5:1) but far below the results in Qiqihar (70:1) and Anguo (96:1).[26]

However lackluster as proselytizers they were, the Americans of the Fushun mission were outstandingly successful pastors. In 1935-36, eighty-seven percent of their followers maintained some active connection with the Church. To a degree this was the result of a conscious decision by the missionaries, who felt constrained by financial necessity and frustrated by Chinese reluctance to convert. In Tonghua, for example, Fr. Escalante worked vigorously to offset the financial difficulties and the lag in converts by revising his program. He redid the one-room catechumenate into a classroom for his government-recognized boys' school. No longer would the mission provide room and board for catechumens. Students from outside the city would have to stay at a local inn unless there were sufficient students in one place to feed and house a catechist. Escalante also managed to have 120

students in his school, one-fourth of them Catholics, given an hour of religious doctrine instruction each day under the cover of an etiquette class. Catholics and catechumens among the student body also received an hour of religious instruction before school officially opened each day; native Sisters taught female students the doctrine. Escalante handled his limited resources well enough to be able in 1934 to provide extensive relief to the victims of a fire which destroyed 300 homes and also to help house those left homeless by a flash flood.[27]

Economics shaped not only the thinking of the priests in the districts but also the concerns of the head of the territory, Raymond A. Lane. The chronic financial plight of his operation moved Lane to consider the example of European Catholic missionaries, who financed many of their activities by speculating in Chinese land. Knowing that James A. Walsh opposed the European method of financing missionary work, Lane nonetheless tried to interest Walsh in land speculation north of booming Dalian. He proposed that the Maryknoll Society enter a partnership with the much-experienced Belgian (Scheut) Fathers. In the expectation of an eight-to-ten percent annual return, Lane would have mortgaged his mission's property to obtain investment capital from a local bank. He argued that by bringing into the deal the Belgians, who were sure to invest in the area anyway and who were the least offensive of the Europeans in their dealings, the Maryknollers would be able to control them and in the event of trouble might be helped by their presence. Later, when his plan became concrete, Lane also attempted to convince James Drought, another Maryknoll official, that investment in a large real estate development along the South Manchurian Railway would double in value within five years.[28]

The head of the Maryknoll Society, James A. Walsh, put an end to Lane's plans. "We dread the reputation of owning revenue producing property," he wrote to Lane, "especially if held, as in China, under the name of the Church, or mission societies." He asked Lane how it would ever be possible to induce the Chinese to support the Church by their sacrifices if they knew that it depended upon business methods. Should that condition arise, the Americans could expect to see in Fushun a replication of what had happened in Manila, where the Catholic people, knowing of the Church's large holdings, refused to tithe or even pay rent to the Church. For the same reason, Walsh announced that Maryknoll would discourage any European society from making investments in any Maryknoll mission area. In his view, the safest method of investment was to purchase stock in a reputable firm whose partners were not identified with the Catholic Church.[29]

Walsh's concern that the Chinese not view the Church as a rich institution linked to the Chinese capitalist class—which it was—paralleled his desire that American benefactors not know the full losses suffered by the Maryknoll Society in China. Walsh's calculating policy generally failed, succeeding only

inasmuch as it saved his society from the gross excesses of other groups. While the Chinese may not have viewed the Maryknoll Society as, for example, a landlord on the grand scale of the Vincentians or the Jesuits, they always viewed the Catholic Church and particularly its American clergy as wealthy.

Without revenue from extensive land speculation or other major investments, the Fushun mission continued to encounter financial difficulties, which dismayed the Maryknoll leadership. Even though the mission had fewer priests, catechists, stations, Catholics, and teachers than the other Maryknoll missions in China except Wuzhou, its expenses were considerably higher. Accordingly, the mission retrenched and paid out less that $8000 for construction in the years 1933-37. Although the Maryknoll leadership agreed to pay $10,000 of the mission's debt in 1935, institutionally the mission was grinding to a halt when the Second Sino-Japanese War broke out.[30]

The Development of Fu Ren University

The development of Fu Ren University contrasts sharply to the setbacks and erosion experienced by the pastoral missions. Under the control of the Fathers of the Society of the Divine Word, Fu Ren reached an enrollment of about 1025 students in January 1935, with a faculty of ninety-seven, including sixty-three lecturers. The percentage of Catholics in the graduating classes grew from nine percent in 1935 to seventeen percent in 1937. In that year, at Fu Ren's seventh graduation exercises, the College of Arts and Letters presented sixty-three candidates for the baccalaureate; the College of Natural Sciences, forty-three; and the College of Education, eighteen. These graduates came from every province of China as well as Mongolia and Manzuguo. In addition to the university work, the Divine Word fathers conducted a boys' middle school and the Sisters Servants of the Holy Spirit operated a girls' middle school. In 1938 the Sisters initiated a college for women at Fu Ren.[31]

The university carried on work of importance to Catholic missionaries. The microbiology laboratory under Dr. Joseph Zhang provided foreign missionaries with vaccine against exanthematous (spotted) typhus, a disease almost invariably fatal to Europeans. In October 1937, Fu Ren established St. Albert's College (Chinese Clerical College) for advanced training for Chinese priests. A School of Chinese Christian Art, directed by its pioneer and dean, Luke Chen, was attempting to develop Chinese artistic expression of Christian themes. There was also a summer school for missionaries and a retreat house to which Chinese Catholic priests, students, and professional men could retire for periods of prayer and consultation on spiritual matters. Moreover, the university maintained a press which published numerous books and documents, the *Fu Jen Sinological Journal* and *Monumenta Serica*, a polyglot journal of oriental studies. There was also an agricultural research program.[32]

The slow progress of Fu Ren University, the setbacks experienced by most missionaries, and the mundane daily mission life did not rouse American Catholics to enthusiastic support of missionary activity. Try though they might to put the best possible face on their societies' mission activity, publicists were hard pressed to find topics which would attract alms. Thus when the Guangdong government settled a mission claim against it by donating to the mission some land where the Jiangmen River entered the South China Sea, Maryknollers led by Joseph Sweeney built a leprosorium there, and the Maryknoll publicist John Considine rejoiced. Considine, who believed that the Church could reach only socially marginal people, welcomed the leprosorium work. As he wrote to the head of the Jiangmen mission: "The blunted apperceptions of the great Catholic public can be aroused only by some such arguments as lepers." Nineteenth-century French missionaries had roused enthusiasm by publicizing their orphanage work but this was offensive to the Chinese. Divine Providence, wrote Considine, seemed to have given the Maryknollers the lepers in order "to awaken poor dull Catholics back home to a realization of the existence of the Church out in Asia."[33]

The outbreak of the Second Sino-Japanese War and its extension into the Pacific War would threaten all of the institutional work of the Church in China and would eventually distract American Catholics so much that they would almost forget the missions. The horror of leprosy and the urge to alleviate its pain were no match for the passions of war.

7

The Gutting and Destruction
of a Battered Church

After the founding of the People's Republic of China in late 1949, many Westerners falsely believed that the Roman Catholic Church in China had been a strong institution until persecuted by the Chinese Communists. Westerners forgot the restrictions, damages, and setbacks inflicted on the Church by the Nationalists as well as the Communists before the Second Sino-Japanese War. They overlooked the devastation inflicted by the Japanese—and in some areas by Chinese and Americans—during the Second Sino-Japanese War; they placed too much reliance on the passing bonds of shared suffering which briefly brought the Western missionaries and some of the Chinese together. And they paid little if any attention to the destruction and disruption experienced at the hands of both sides during the Nationalist-Communist Civil War. In fact, the Communist regime merely pushed over the battered shell of an internally troubled institution that both Nationalists and Communists had mauled before the Japanese gutted it.

The Gutting of the Roman Catholic Church in China

The invading Japanese attempted to destroy Christianity in China. They attacked mission stations and hospitals, often forbade church services and religious teaching, and restricted the movement of missionaries. After the outbreak of war with the United States, they interned all the American missionaries they could capture and drove the rest into hiding. Their military operations resulted in the death of Christians, scattered Christian congregations, made routine pastoral care impossible, and worsened the financial condition of many missionaries to the point that missionary activity became impossible and the missionaries despaired.

The Second Sino-Japanese War grew out of the great social and economic problems of Japan's status as a competitive capitalist society. To alleviate those problems, the Japanese leadership wanted to preserve and even monopolize China as a weak, exploitable nation. But in December 1936, when Jiang's subordinates forced their leader to abandon his war against the Communists and form a united front against further Japanese encroachment, the growth of Chinese political and military power became a distinct possibility. The Japanese attacked before China could gather its full strength.

The eight-year-long war began with a minor incident on July 7, 1937, at the Marco Polo Bridge ten miles west of Beijing. The invaders moved quickly and took Beijing on July 28, 1937. Then they fought their way down the Beijing-Wuhan railway and took over Xinxiang, where the American Divine Word Fathers maintained a central mission station. To the east, in Shandong, they captured Zhoucun, principal focus of the American Franciscans' Zibo mission, in December 1937. By year's end they held nearly all the major cities of northern China and that region's railway and communications systems.

One by one, the Japanese military occupied the American Catholic mission areas in northern and central China. After Zhoucun, the Japanese took Kaifeng, where the Sisters of Providence and American Benedictine priests and Sisters worked. Then Hanyang, where the Sisters of Loretto worked, fell to the aggressors; then Wuchang, vicariate apostolic of the Cincinnati province Franciscans; and finally, in June 1940, Shashi, the center of the New York Province Franciscans' district.

The Japanese also launched attacks on the southern coastal area of China; once they had a foothold there, they conducted an aerial war against the South China interior. In late 1937, the Japanese shelled Chiqi, in the Jiangmen, Guangdong, vicariate apostolic and drove the resident missionary into the hills. They took over Xiachuan Island and the Maryknoll Sisters there withdrew to Hong Kong. As Chinese defense forces destroyed the roads to slow the Japanese, transportation deteriorated and travel became difficult for the missionaries. The Japanese regained their momentum and pressed ahead, bombing Luoding, wounding Fr. Kennelly, and dispersing the population from the towns into the villages where it was difficult for the relatively old Jiangmen Maryknollers to reach them. In March 1939, they captured Jiangmen, where the mission compound was a refuge for hundreds of Chinese.[1]

Japanese planes conducted a terror-bombing campaign against the unoccupied areas of China. Despite warnings from U.S. consular officials, many missionaries remained at their stations and some narrowly escaped death. The Japanese bombed the Jian'ou, Fujian, mission station of the American Dominicans on June 25, 1939. The constant air raids against the American Vincentians' Ganzhou, Jiangxi, territory, seriously disrupted missionary work during this same period. In Yudu, Jiangxi, for example, air raid alerts sent the priests running for shelter almost daily.[2]

The Passionists' territory in Hunan province suffered very heavily from the air attacks. In April 1940, Japanese planes bombed the Passionists' mission at Zhijiang, inflicting $1000 damage. They damaged the Zhijiang mission again on September 4, 1940, and that same day bombed the Passionists' mission at Chenxi. Thereupon, the American ambassador to Japan, Joseph Grew, urged Washington to take steps to prevent a recurrence of similar attacks. But the Japanese attacks on American Catholic missions, including those of the Passionists, continued. On September 9, 1940, the Japanese airmen attacked the mission at Luqi, causing $1000 damage. The Japanese Foreign Office subsequently expressed its regret for the Luqi incident but added that since Japanese troops had not occupied the area, it was unable to investigate the circumstances of the attack. On May 7, 1941, Japanese pilots destroyed the Yuanling mission's convent, high school, and primary schools. The Japanese consul general at Shanghai expressed his regrets but claimed that the proximity of the property to munition-laden junks on the Yuan River made it inevitable that it would receive "a few stray bombs."[3]

The Japanese continued their terror-bombing campaign against the Chinese as well as Westerners in China. The Catholic missions continued to absorb losses. On August 15, 1941, the invaders bombed the Dominicans' Jian'ou station and caused some damage. Then on November 25, 1941, Japaneses aviators made five direct hits on the Longnan mission station in the Vincentians' Ganzhou, Jiangxi, mission territory. They killed the gatekeeper, a catechist, and ten of the one hundred refugees in the mission and seriously wounded twenty other refugees. Fortunately, the children in the mission's schools were off on their annual autumn outing.[4]

Japanese Restrictions on the Missions

Behind Japanese lines, American Catholic missionaries found their movement and activities restricted. Japanese officials claimed that these restrictions were for the safety of third-country nationals who insisted on remaining in bandit-ridden territory. (Often the so-called bandits were guerrillas.) In late 1937, after bandits in the Fushun, Manzuguo, territory kidnapped and eventually murdered the Maryknoll priest Gerard Donovan, the missionaries there found that existing Japanese restrictions on their movement were being tightened. The bishops of Manzuguo cooperated by permitting their priests to visit sick people only with the prior permission of the police. The Fushun mission superior restricted the Maryknoll Sisters to visits in the city and the priests had to seek ways to attract Catholics and catechumens to the mission compounds.[5]

As relations between Japan and the United States deteriorated in the summer of 1941, the United States choked off Japanese financial credit in the

United States. The Japanese government retaliated with new and very stringent travel regulations for non-Japanese foreigners in Manzuguo and Japanese-occupied China. By law they might travel on the first, eleventh, and twenty-first day of the month with prior permission, which was sometimes not given. This made it almost impossible to visit the mission outstations. The Japanese police in Fushun went further and closed three outstations, allowing them to be reopened only when the American consul protested. The Japanese were merely biding their time. Thus when one Maryknoll missionary arrived at Xinbin in September 1941, the Japanese police chief told him he was wasting his time—the Catholic Church had no future in Manzuguo. That was true of all Japanese-occupied China.[6]

American Catholic missionaries encountered more restrictions than those on their movements. The religious laws of Manzuguo, which gave the missionaries official status, made it difficult for them not only to change personnel from one station to another but also to open new stations. Equally troublesome was the very strict enforcement by the Japanese of a prohibition against the teaching of religion in the mission schools. The Japanese forbade the missionaries in Manzuguo to close the religionless mission schools and thus forced the financially hard-pressed mission to run nonsectarian public schools. Far to the south, in Guangdong, the invaders ordered the missionaries in the seminary conducted by Maryknoll priests to stop using certain history books and all Mandarin-dialect books in the seminary and to obtain new books published by the puppet government.[7]

The cumulative Japanese restrictions and the wartime dangers caused some church authorities to question the wisdom of attempting to maintain mission operations at their prewar level. Monsignor Julius Dillon, O.F.M., head of the American Franciscan mission in Shashi, for example, sent half of his personnel home to America in February 1941, and called in Belgian Franciscans to operate the central mission station in Shashi. The American Franciscans who remained worked in the countryside as far as possible from the Japanese.[8]

With the outbreak of war between Japan and the United States, Japanese authorities in most areas of occupied China sought to arrest and intern the local American Catholic missionaries. The Japanese authorities in Zibo, Shandong, area, however, were very slow to round up the local American priests and Sisters and waited until March 21, 1943, before they arrested the Americans and interned them. In the interim, the Sisters had supplied Communist guerrillas with medicine. Fourteen of the Zibo area's nineteen priests and some of its Sisters were repatriated in September 1943.[9]

A few Americans managed to escape the Japanese dragnet and became fugitives. Some of them slipped into unoccupied China while others preferred to continue working in the remote countryside where they ran the risk of capture by the Japanese or their collaborators. On November 29, 1942,

Japanese troops captured Fr. Ralph Knopke, O.F.M., who was working in the rural areas of the Shashi mission territory. They then burned his church and imprisoned him on the charge that he was an advisor to a local guerrilla leader. The continued presence of three fugitive Franciscans in the same territory so infuriated the Japanese that they burned down the church at Beijizhou, destroyed the mission compounds at Zhangjinhe and Hexue, and shelled the church at Shadaguan.[10]

The Missionaries' War Relief Work

As the Japanese advanced into China, the missionaries were inundated with refugees and wounded Chinese soldiers. The Americans threw open the gates of their mission compounds and hospitals to the unfortunates and put aside their normal pastoral and educational services to care for the Chinese. In Kaifeng, Henan, for example, the missionaries in the city helped to organize an International Relief Committee under the leadership of Fr. Francis Clougherty, now back in Kaifeng as a Benedictine priest and head of Henan University's Department of English. In early April 1938, the Benedictines, the Providence Sisters, and the Sisters Catechists joined other church people in caring for the wounded Chinese soldiers who were being shipped by the trainload from the battlefield to rear areas. The missionaries met every train for eight weeks, helping to care for more than 50,000 wounded. The Franciscan missionaries in Shashi, using government funds in addition to their own, fed more than 2000 daily for over three months and cared for thousands of wounded Chinese.[11]

American Catholic relief work lasted longer in areas which the Japanese did not capture early in the war. In Fujian the Dominicans were conducting war relief as late as 1943. In western Hunan, which became a refugee center shortly after the outbreak of the war, the Passionists undertook extensive relief work. By 1940 they were operating twelve refugee camps with 10,182 registered refugees; they also maintained two relief hospitals which treated 156,227 outpatients. The missioners also cared for and fed 1552 bombing victims.[12]

The missionaries' relief work took the edge off the suspicion and hatred which many Chinese felt toward the Catholic Church's representatives. The experience of the Divine Word Society missionaries in Xinxiang confirmed this lessening of chronic ill-feeling toward them and the institution they represented. Upon the outbreak of fighting between Japan and the United States, the attitude of many Chinese toward the Americans became less hostile and even, on occasion, warm. Fleeing from Japanese-occupied territory, the head of Maryknoll's Jiangmen mission, Adolph Paschang, received assistance not only from Chinese troops employed by the Japanese and Chinese guerillas but also from Chinese bandits. Commenting on the changed sentiment among the Chinese, Paschang wrote, "In the ordinary course of events some of those hideouts would be places for a certain plucking, but with the proper passwords all men are brothers." The anti-Japanese feeling and the shared dangers of war thus provided a temporary bridge spanning the chasm between the relatively wealthy Americans and the Chinese, something which the Christian gospel had not done at other times.[13]

While the relief work continued, crowded mission compounds and camps provided the setting for unprecedented interest in Catholicism and exceptionally large numbers of Chinese converts. These developments occurred perhaps because Chinese and Americans shared a common peril, considered themselves allies, and were together for long periods of time. Furthermore, the missionaries, who never made religious belief a condition for receipt of aid, were offering an alternative belief system in a uniquely appropriate setting at a time when war had completely disrupted traditional patterns. Under such circumstances, for example, the Franciscans in Zibo twice ran out of catechisms when their territory was a battle zone and their mission compounds were crowded with refugees. Similarly, 1941 was the best year in the history of the Passionist mission. The Passionists recorded more than 1000 adult conversions that year.[14]

The relief work absorbed the energies and funds of the missionaries; the financial burden which it imposed became acute even before the outbreak of hostilities between the United States and Japan. In late winter and early spring of 1940, the cost of providing a rice dole for refugees became so great that Adolph Paschang, second Maryknoll leader of the Jiangmen, Guangdong, vicariate apostolic, asked Maryknoll headquarters for permission to make direct appeals to American Catholics for help in refugee work. The superior general of Maryknoll turned down Paschang's request for three reasons. He did not want missioners in the field working outside of the Maryknoll Society's established channels. He did not want to offend the Japanese authorities as several Protestant groups had done. "We must keep in mind our duties toward those Maryknollers who have to carry out their apostolic vocation under the Japanese flag," he wrote. Finally, he did not want any Maryknollers responsible for such funds. With hundreds of agencies attempting to raise funds for the Chinese refugees, he wondered "just how much of these charitable donations reach their proper destination, especially since the American Chinese and Chinese students have not a little to do with gathering them."[15]

This last reason advanced by the Maryknoll Society's chief was consistent with two strains in the mission leader's thought: a distrust of and disdain for the Chinese people and also a fear that church workers might be tainted by association with disreputable characters. This same superior, when head of the Jiangmen mission, had forbidden Fr. George Bauer to visit two towns in the Dianbai district known for gambling and prostitution. Indeed, under his leadership the mission had kept a certain distance from the local Chinese (Catholics included), people he adjudged "unpromising types," and generally shiftless people living in the most disorganized region of China's most disorganized province. Instead, the mission had turned inward, conserving its resources while preparing for "great future battles." Relief work was only a temporary reorientation of the Jiangmen mission activity and although it expressed the deep humanitarian feelings of the missionaries, it did not eradicate their lingering suspicion of the people they assisted.[16]

The Chasm between the Missionaries and the Chinese

The chasm between missionaries and Chinese was always visible to those who cared to look over the side of the flimsy bridge provided by wartime camaraderie. In the Yujiang, Jiangxi, mission, Monsignor Misner admitted that only the war drew the American and Chinese clergy together, a task he was unable to accomplish on his own. While Misner was unhappy with four of the ten American missionaries in his extensive territory because they did not have a grasp of the language and were "quite content to speak very imperfectly and will make no effort as long as they can make themselves partially understood," he had even less respect for most of his Chinese clergy. "The best that can be expected from the natives is that they do not cause trouble," he wrote, "They show very little zeal for the conversion of their fellows."[17]

In the adjoining Ganzhou vicariate apostolic during 1938, the head of that territory, Monsignor O'Shea, removed the priests from Dawoli and put the district under ecclesiastical interdict (deprivation of the sacraments) until the Christians there bowed to the will of the local priests and allowed them to run the mission as they saw fit. Just as Eastern European Catholic immigrants to the United States had finally accepted complete priestly authority over the material affairs of the local Catholic churches, so the Catholics in Dawoli grudgingly accepted the same arrangement and the bishop of Ganzhou lifted his ban. When the priests finally returned to Dawoli, however, few Christians came to the mission. Adverting to the affair, a priest wrote, "Would you call it Nationalism? I think that is what they call it in the States when the Poles, Checks [sic], Lithuanians or other foreign bodies try to run the Church."[18]

The estrangement of the missionaries from the Christians of Dawoli was only one manifestation of their loss of contact with Chinese Catholics and with the Chinese in general. In 1940–41, the number of Christians decreased by about 700. The draft and draft evasion, disregard of marriage laws by Christians, and the lack of money to run "eating" schools all contributed to the disintegration of the church structure. The priests debated whether to use catechumenates or schools to reach the Chinese, but by late 1941 the debate was academic on two counts: the vicariate apostolic lacked the money to operate catechumenates, and opening schools to attract students entailed government registration yet a government-approved school would attract so many non-Christians that those students would try to dictate school policy.[19]

Finally, after December 1941, the old tensions between Church and nationalistic state, as well as wartime hardship, hastened the decline of the Ganzhou mission. Local Chinese Catholic children attended public schools (as required by law) and drifted out of contact with the missionaries. In the outlying areas the hard-pressed Christians were seemingly no longer interested in religion; just making a living was difficult and time-consuming enough. A local Vincentian observing developments in unoccupied China was concerned that the Chinese state was reaching for an all-encompassing authority that could only restrict the church. He lamented that "the young men are herded into the army . . . the children herded into the public schools . . . the women herded into the fields to work . . . and the end is not yet."[20]

In striking contrast to the typical Ganzhou mission territory was the atypical adjacent mission in Mei Xian, Guangdong, operated by the Maryknoll Fathers under Monsignor Francis X. Ford. Although the Japanese did bomb some cities in the district, including Mei Xian, their troops never entered the mountainous area and the Maryknoll personnel were able to proceed with their mission work. In 1940 the mission began publishing a monthly magazine, *Sin Nam Sen*. In 1941 the priests were celebrating Mass in 280 stations in the territory; in 1942 they added fifteen stations to their circuits. In the same two-year span the number of local Catholics grew from 18,924 to 19,397, three times the Catholic population when Ford had begun the Maryknoll effort in Mei Xian seventeen years before.[21]

Elsewhere in China, American Catholic mission efforts suffered substantial damage as a result of the war. In Beijing, Fu Jen University lost half its student enrollment when the Japanese invaded. But because the university curriculum emphasized science and because the presence of a German rector afforded some political protection, Fu Ren attracted teachers and students in greater numbers than ever before and became a center of Chinese nationalism. Nonetheless, when the Japanese arrested the university's American faculty members after December 7, 1941, they dealt the university a severe blow.[22]

In western Hunan, the outbreak of fighting between Japan and the United States complicated an already difficult financial situation for the Passionists and the Sisters who worked with them, making it difficult for the missionaries to obtain funds from the United States. Some of the priests eked out their existence as contract chaplains in the U.S. Army in China. In Fujian, too, the American Dominicans had almost exhausted their funds and by 1943 half their mission was closed. No mail from the provincial superior of the Americans had reached them since April 1941, and of this lack of personal encouragement, Fr. B.C. Werner lamented, "It is crushing my spirits and the spirits of all."[23]

While the Maryknoll Mei Xian mission escaped the direct effects of the war, the Maryknoll missions in Jiangmen, Wuzhou, and Gueilin (detached in 1938 from the Wuzhou mission) suffered severely. Adolph Paschang, leader of the Jiangmen mission, reported in 1941 that most of the stations in his mission had sustained heavy, in some cases irreparable, property damage from Japanese bombing. Pastoral conditions were similar to those in the Vincentian missions in Jiangxi. No one had time for religion. He noted that mission "activity is limited practically to trying to hold onto what we have; even that is hard these days when everybody is absorbed in trying to get enough money to buy a pound of rice."[24]

The Japanese inflicted still more damage and disruption upon the missions in late 1944 and 1945 when they attempted to link occupied areas along the China coast and to move far enough inland to destroy the large American airbases which were the key to anti-Japanese operations in South China. Missionary priests and Sisters fled from the advancing Japanese in Hunan, Guangdong, and Guangxi. The Maryknollers who did not hide in the hills often sought refuge in Kunming, Yunnan. The Vincentian missions in Jiangxi suffered more than $2,500,000 in damages and personal property loss.[25]

On a visit to China in late 1944 and 1945, the head of the Maryknoll Society found that some of his men had already left China for India and the United States. Of the seventy-six who remained in China, six were interned; eight were serving as contract chaplains and a ninth was awaiting his appointment as a chaplain; two were teaching at Fudan University in Chongqing (Chungking); one was waiting for his passport to leave China; six were thoroughly demoralized and at least five of the six left for the United States in January 1945. Most of the rest of the priests were encircled by the Japanese and were still trying to carry out their missionary task. The war had thus reduced the number of Maryknoll priests and Brothers in China to half of the 151 in China in October 1941.[26]

The reduction in the number of active missionaries did not daunt the Maryknoll leader. He stressed in a report of his visit: "N.B. Enough missioners remain on hand to administer both Kuelin [Guelin] and Wuchow [Wuzhou] missions in case of re-entry. Many compounds in both missions are destroyed and it will not be necessary or practical to send large squads of men back to either place at once."[27] Thus the Japanese gutted the American Catholic missions and the rest of the Roman Catholic Church in China.

The Redirection of American Catholic Missionary Effort

When the war reduced the size of their contingents in China and cut or diminished their ties with those that remained, the mission-sending societies began to protect themselves from the sudden loss of employment opportunities for their members. The Maryknoll Society, as the largest of the American Catholic China mission groups, was the most affected by the disruption of World War II and would have been greatly threatened by the loss of access to China had it not begun shortly after the attack on Pearl Harbor to find other outlets for its men. Full of would-be missionaries, the society embarked on a headlong expansion during the years 1942–48. In 1942, the society opened missions in the Huehuetenango prelature and Guatemala City archdiocese, Guatemala; in the Cochabamba diocese, La Paz archdiocese, Pando vicariate apostolic, and Santa Cruz diocese, Bolivia; and in the Merida archdiocese, and Tepic diocese, Mexico (closed, 1946). In 1943, the society opened missions in the Talca, Temuco and Chillan dioceses, Chile; in the Lima archdiocese and Puno diocese, Peru, and in the Guayaquil diocese, Ecuador (closed, 1946). In 1946, the society opened missions in the Musoma diocese, Tanzania, and Pusan diocese, Korea. In 1948, it expanded into the Mexico City archdiocese. This rapid expansion into new mission areas, occasionally with individual priests, usually in bands of two to seven, served the same institutional function as expansion into Guangxi had served twenty years before: it relieved the pressure on the society to find mission fields for its men at minimal risk to itself.

The head of the Maryknoll organization had as little respect for the Latin Americans as he had for the Chinese. He noted of the Latin people, "Many vices, few spiritual virtues and no vocations"; of Latin Catholicism, "pious women, careless men, neglected children and sacristy clergy"; and of Latin men, "angels up to the end of school age, worldly and negligent nitwits from then on." In a similarly disdainful way he noted of the Chinese, "I doubt if any person who has lived in China can ever be surprised or dismayed at any sort of conditions existing, for when it comes to dark ways, vain tricks and double-barreled trouble, the Chinese can give cards and spades to the rest of the world."[28]

Planning for the Future of the China Missions

Notwithstanding the turbulent history of the China missions, the attraction of other mission fields, and the disdain for the Chinese people, the head of the Maryknoll Society and a few other mission leaders were encouraged about the future of the China missions. After years of frustration by antiforeignism, the Maryknoll leader wrote of a better future based on the friendliness of a key Nationalist Chinese leader, T. V. Song. The Passionist Cuthbert O'Gara announced to his confreres that "a new China is being born and a new future is opening up to the Missions in the Far East." His prescription for success in the "new China" was better prepared missionaries and additional financial support. The Divine Word mission leader Thomas Megan emphasized medical work and more efficient organization as the key to future success in the Xinxiang mission.[29]

The planning of these mission leaders ignored fundamental questions about the future of the China missions. The Sino-American camaraderie fostered by the war quickly dissipated and Chinese nationalism emerged to haunt the missionaries where it had the greatest immediate effect, within the Church itself. As these intangible problems mounted, so did the tangible difficulties posed by the civil war between the Nationalist and Communist parties.

The Negative Impact of American Military Operations

American military operations in China dissipated some of the good feelings of the Chinese for the United States and both directly and indirectly harmed American Catholic missionary efforts. During the war and immediately thereafter close cooperation existed between the United States military and many American Catholic missionaries, but United States bombing inflicted damage on some American Catholic missions and increased the underlying tensions between Americans and Chinese. Thomas Megan, who worked against Japan as an army chaplain and OSS collaborator, for example, returned to Xinxiang, Henan, to find that three American bombs had destroyed the main mission building. The American pattern bombing of Hanyang, Wuhan, and Wuchang stirred up anger and bitterness among the Chinese, including Chinese Catholic Sisters. The loose moral behavior of the U.S. troops embarrassed the missionaries, particularly those serving as chaplains, a role forced upon some priests by poverty but one which soon became a liability. The Passionist missionary-turned-chaplain Fr. Regis Boyle said of the servicemen's behavior: "The serviceman in general has gone to hell here in the Orient—less than 15% [of the Catholics] even go to Mass, and that by exact survey." Clearly unable to command the respect and obedience of American Catholics, the missionaries were thus less able to command the respect and obedience of Chinese Catholics.[30]

The Passionist bishop Cuthbert O'Gara quietly drew attention to an event which he felt was the most important in the erosion of the moral authority of American Catholic missionaries, and Americans in general, in China: the dropping of the atomic bomb on Japan. Speaking to the Third Annual Conference of the strongly anti-Communist Cardinal Mindszenty Foundation, O'Gara recounted an incident during his captivity by the Chinese Communists which changed his assessment of American moral authority. In the midst of a lecture on the evils of imperialism, O'Gara attempted to defend the U.S. government by recalling its foreign aid programs. "You Americans boast that you are the world's unquestioned do-gooders and glad-handers," retorted his interrogator, "and you smugly take for granted that your professions of good fellowship must everywhere be taken at face value. Who dropped the first atomic bomb?" O'Gara told his audience, "It was as if a streak of lightning had struck. In that blinding instant I saw what I had never realized before—that at Hiroshima, Oh! the tragedy of it! America had lost the moral leadership of the world. You may be sure of this. In every tea-house of the Orient and in every coffee-bar of the Near East, Hiroshima and all it signifies, is a perennial topic of conversation. . . . Hiroshima today is like the 'damned spot' that MacBeth struggled so frantically to banish from his mind."[31]

Nationalism among the Chinese Catholic Clergy

The erosion of American moral authority intensified the nationalism of the Chinese Catholic clergy. Feelings against Americans and foreigners in general were strong among the Chinese clergy, confident of their ability to run the Catholic Church in China and insistent on doing so. That insistence soon became well publicized and a source of discomfiture to the foreign missionaries. Although the Vatican's chief representative in China, the Papal Internuncio, called for concord between foreign and domestic clergy, Chinese clergy demanded that the Vatican establish a Chinese hierarchy. The Vatican complied in 1946.

The Vatican's establishment of the Chinese hierarchy indicated who would govern the Church in China, set a seal of approval on the nationalistic feelings of the Chinese clergy, and marked the end of the heyday of Catholic foreign missionaries in China. Even though the missionaries had contributed much to this stage in the history of the Roman Catholic Church in China, many of them, out of disdain for the Chinese, fear for their jobs and authority, or fear of change, found it difficult to accept. One Maryknoller reported from Tianjin (Tientsin) in August 1947, "I have heard time and again here in Tientsin—the big danger to the Church in China is not the Communists, but the native clergy."[32]

The future of the Roman Catholic Church in China would be decided by the outcome of a struggle between two political groups which had a history of animosity toward the Church rather than by the outcome of an ecclesiastical power struggle. The civil war between the Nationalists and the Communists was attended by the deaths of multitudes and the devastation of wide areas. Both sides inflicted heavy losses on the Church during the course of the war.

Two Troubles: Civil War and Communism

After the defeat of Japan, the question of who would rule China came immediately to the fore. The main actors who would settle the issue were

Chinese; Americans, as usual, played only a subsidiary role in the unfolding of events. Certainly American policy makers wished to see China emerge as a stable counterweight to Russia and Japan in Northeast Asia but they could not dictate the course of history. The American leaders could not persuade American citizens to engage in a war in China for the nebulous reasons of realpolitik. Nonetheless, they meddled in the civil war on behalf of the Nationalists just as the British and French had sided with the Manchus against the Taipings almost a century before. The Americans provided the Nationalists with logistical support, a protective force of U.S. Marines in North China, and, through the United Nations Relief and Rehabilitation Administration (UNRRA), hundreds of millions of dollars in relief supplies and materiel to rebuild China's railroads, some key industries, and agriculture. Just as some missionaries had cooperated with the British and French against the Taipings, so some missionaries cooperated with the UNRRA program.

The war went badly for the Nationalists after an initial year of success. The United States flew three Nationalist armies to key areas of North and East China before the Communists could occupy them. Some 50,000 U.S. Marines assisted the Nationalists in occupying Beijing, Tianjin, and the key coal mining and transportation facilities in that area. The Nationalists moved into Manchuria before they had established control over Central China. Overextended and committed to positional warfare, the Nationalist forces lost the initiative in Manchuria by the end of 1946.

In Manchuria and elsewhere the Communists built their strength for battles soon to come. Within a year the Communists had isolated the Nationalists in Manchuria and in the spring of 1948 took several cities in Central China, including Kaifeng. By September 1948, Nationalist troops had lost the will to fight and the Communists achieved important victories in Shandong. The Nationalists lost Manchuria shortly thereafter. By the end of January 1949, the Communists had taken Beijing without a fight. In late April 1949, the Communists crossed the Chang Jiang (Yangtze) and in late May they took Shanghai. Within a few more months they had effective control of the mainland while most of the remaining Nationalist forces were digging in on Taiwan, an island pacified by the Nationalists in 1947 after a popular uprising against the mainlanders.

Some American Catholic missions sustained heavy damage during the civil war. The Maryknoll Fushun mission suffered damage to ten chapels, ten rectories, four convents, a seminary, and five other buildings. As late as February 1947, there were only four Maryknoll priests in the mission; by January 1948, all but two had fled the sprawling mission territory. In the Zibo, Shandong, mission an American Franciscan priest noted, "This civil war has certainly been a set-back for the missions. Whole villages of newly baptized Christians (especially the Pochuang [Bozhuang] district) have fallen away. Many villages have not seen a priest for one or more years. Chiangchia [Jiangjia] has not seen a priest for a year and a half." The same priest observed that the Communists found the peasantry receptive to their claims that all religion was nonsense, the invention of foreigners. The Communists had become so numerous and strong in the northern part of the mission that the Adorers of the Blood of Christ, a nursing and teaching group that had been stationed there before internment by the Japanese, found it impossible to return and were recalled to the United States by their Mother Superior before the end of 1945. Both Nationalists and Communists inflicted so much damage on mission property in Zibo and Zhoucun during the following year that a Franciscan priest advised his fellow missionaries on leave in the United States not to return to Shandong. Finally, in February 1947, as the Communists approached Zibo and Zhoucun yet again, the American Franciscans abandoned their mission territory and a week later some of them left China.[33]

The American Divine Word Fathers' Xinxiang, Henan, mission also suffered through civil war and communism. When Thomas Megan's society was slow to send reinforcements after his return to Xinxiang in October 1945, he went to work with a handful of American and German priests to step up the mission's school program and particularly its hospital program. He also recruited missionaries from other areas. When his supply of medicines failed to meet the needs of the mission's six hospitals and large clinics, he set up a pharmaceutical company. But progress in the mission was offset by losses sustained in the western part of the mission territory when Communist troops looted the mission stations there in late 1945. As the local military balance shifted against the Nationalists and the Communists advanced, the missionaries fled from one station to another and by April 1947, the cost of shifting personnel had bankrupted the mission. With twenty-two years of uninterrupted work in China behind him, Megan returned to the United States to raise money for the mission. In July 1948, he learned that the Vatican had removed him from the leadership of the mission. He never returned to China but instead began missionary work among black Americans in Hattiesburg, Mississippi, where he quietly challenged local racial segregation and integrated his parish.[34]

The Dominican Jian'ou, Fujian, mission also suffered badly as a result of the civil war. Communist guerrillas killed Fr. James Devine in May 1947. By July 1948, there were only four American Dominican priests and a group of American Dominican Sisters in Jian'ou, the smallest mission in Fujian and the third from the smallest in China. In late April 1949, the Sisters left at the command of their Mother Superior. Events demonstrated that the command was prudent. Retreating Nationalists behaved so badly in the area that the works of the mission came to a standstill and Paul Curran was moved to write from Jian'ou, "The Ex-President [Jiang] says that in three years they will again be back in Nanking. In the meanwhile the thousands killed, robberies, rapes and the many other injustices following an army never seems to enter their heads. It burns me up to see how they are honored in the USA, seeing how little they care for their own people or foreigners in this country."[35]

The crumbling Nationalist regime squeezed the people ever harder for conscripts and money, destroying in the process what was left of its political base. To relieve the human suffering and to save the Nationalist regime from its own depradations, public and private relief agencies in the capitalist world stepped up work in China. The main relief agency was the United Nations Relief and Rehabilitation Agency (UNRRA), which drew most of its support and direction from the United States government.

UNRRA established headquarters in Guangzhou (Canton) in early 1946. Several months later, the Catholic Church established the headquarters of its United States-based Catholic Relief Services (CRS) in Guangzhou. The Maryknoll priest Paul J. Duchesne had the responsibility for establishing and maintaining CRS liaison with UNRRA. Working with him was another Maryknoll priest, Francis O'Neill. Duchesne found that UNRRA workers were skeptical of the missionaries' usefulness and reluctant to hire them. Furthermore, some churchmen were diffident about involvement with UNRRA. One French bishop expressed the opinion that UNRRA was a way of opening China to U.S. business. As a result of the mutual distrust, although UNRRA used many missions as distribution points, few Catholic missionaries worked for UNRRA and those who did soon tired of the corruption of the program and longed to return to their usual pastoral routines.[36]

Foreign assistance to the disintegrating Nationalist regime did not long delay the Communist victory. After more than a decade of war and despoliation, the Chinese people were willing to accept any Chinese government which would bring peace and order. By 1949, if not before, the Nationalist government had shown itself unable to do so and its leaders left for Taiwan in 1949 and 1950. A Communist government was the only alternative.

In many war-torn areas, the arrival of the Communist troops was abetted by the local people, including Chinese Catholics. The Archbishop of Fuzhou, the Dominican T. Labrador, tried to explain this to the Provincial Superior of the American Dominicans by saying that many Christians had joined the Communists out of hunger and ignorance. The physical safety of the missionaries increased after the restoration of order by the Communists. In Guangxi some Maryknollers found that Red Army troops were friendly. The Passionists in the Yuanling area of Hunan experienced the same phenomenon.[37]

Generally, the arrival of party cadre changed for the worse the conditions under which the missionaries lived and the outbreak of the Korean War made them worse still. In Guangxi, the Maryknoller Herbert Elliott found that in secret Communist civilian officials were sympathetic, even apologetic to the missionaries, but their public behavior was unfriendly and mean. In Guangdong, the Maryknoller Robert Kennelly found local Communist officials to be friendly, but after the outbreak of the Korean War, hostile officials arrived from outside the area and began persecuting the missionaries. Typically, party cadres encouraged local criticism of the missionaries, kept them under surveillance, and discouraged Christians from visiting the churches. The antireligious activities of the party cadre and government officials were reminiscent of the Nationalists' similar activity during the 1920s and gave the lie to promises of freedom of religion granted in Article Three of the Common Program of the People's Republic of China adopted in September 1949.[38]

The domestic and international problems of the new regime could not have encouraged it to allow the missionaries and their followers to operate in their usual fashion. The Nationalists, with support from the U.S. government, were still fighting a guerrilla war on the mainland of China. The U.S. government was not only supporting a French colonial war in Indochina, on China's southern border, but it was also involved in a war in Korea on China's northeastern border, a war that soon involved the Chinese. As for the American Catholic missionaries, many had a wartime record of collaboration with Nationalist and American military forces. Some were also chronic violators of the currency regulations meant to stabilize the war-ravaged economy and preserve national economic strength. Moreover, all of the missionaries had ties with the Vatican, which was then collaborating with the capitalist nations, especially the United States, in a general anti-Communist crusade.

The Beijing government systematically reduced the institutional church. Land reform in 1951 stripped the church of its rural holdings, including mission chapels and stations. By the end of 1952 the government had taken over all but a few scattered educational institutions belonging to the church. The missionaries themselves experienced very tight travel restrictions and some of them were jailed. The government subjected many of the jailed missionaries to harsh interrogation, some to years of solitary confinement, a few to physical brutality. The captors of F.X. Ford beat him to death.

The jailed missionaries were able to observe the new regime at close hand. Cuthbert O'Gara became convinced that the Communist Party was modeled on the organizational pattern of the Catholic hierarchy and that much Communist doctrine was drawn from Catholic sources. His captors' practice of meditation on Communist truths, as well as their attendance at lectures on Communism and at a ten-day retreat, struck him forcibly. "I would walk up and down the narrow confines of my cell and reflect how much all of this was like to the ultra-fervent conduct of the Founder and first companions of a Religious Order or Congregation." Other missionaries were struck by the similarity between their prison routine with its interrogation and propaganda sessions, often referred to as "brainwashing," and their experience in the seminary.[39]

Expulsion

The regime found it easier to deal with the missionaries than with their Chinese followers. It expelled the missionaries over a period that extended down to 1956. A lone American Catholic missionary, James E. Walsh, lingered in Guangzhou, was arrested in 1958, and was imprisoned for more than a decade. But Chinese Catholics, stripped of their ties to the foreigners, insisted on practicing their religion and though their numbers declined sharply, the regime was not able to eradicate Roman Catholicism quickly.

8

Partners in Semicolonialism

The Taiping Rebellion and other chronic rebellions of the mid-nineteenth century were the first compelling evidence that Chinese society was disintegrating, and the grip of its Manchu overlords weakening. Furthermore, the presence of hostile foreigners with superior technology and organization made it clear even to the bureaucratic custodians of the old Confucian order that some innovations in Chinese society were necessary. So the last of the Manchu rulers tried to graft Western technology and governmental patterns onto the old culture. The foreign powers were willing to cooperate with this process in order to save the Manchus, because it was easier to exploit China through its relatively weak government than to quarrel over its division or to police its millions. This mode of exploitation earned the name "semicolonialism."

Partners in Semicolonialism

During those troubled years of the mid-nineteenth century, Western Christian missionaries, Roman Catholic and Protestant, forced their way into China. The foreign churchmen were close to both the Manchu government and the foreign powers. The Jesuits, for example, acted as interpreters and quartermasters for Western forces assisting the Manchus to put down the Taiping rebels. After a few Protestant missionaries flirted with the Taipings, the representatives of Protestantism also cooperated with the central government. At the beginning of the twentieth century, Catholic missionaries took the next step and assumed through treaty the rank and privileges of Chinese officials.

Protestant and Roman Catholic missionaries generally followed different strategies in China. Protestant church workers concentrated most of their energies in the cities and towns where a new social order was beginning to arise. Through their schools they sought to influence the emerging bourgeois and petit bourgeois classes. Their contribution to the Chinese reform movement was significant. From the beginning of the twentieth century when they undertook English-medium education on a large scale, their influence grew. Roman Catholic missionaries, on the other hand, spread through the interior of the country where they concentrated on converting the peasantry, often by meddling in the law courts on behalf of actual or prospective clients.

The concentration of Catholic mission work in the rural areas reflected the inability of Catholicism to deal with the nascent capitalist society of the treaty ports. The missioners felt that the Roman Church was ill-adapted to deal with life in the port cities, and during the twentieth century they came to fear that rural society would become like that in the ports. A rural peasantry transformed into a farming society linked to international, national, or regional economies was a discouraging prospect. The Maryknoll leader of the Jiangmen mission gave voice to these fears when he observed in 1929, "In general our feeling is that we have not come too late, but we must get sharply to work—with China on the eve of modernization as it appears to be. We must reap a harvest before our country people take on the sophistication and worldliness of our city populations for the problem of establishing the Church among the latter class is a difficult one, and one not satisfactorily solved, as far as our knowledge goes, by any mission in China."[1]

The Powers behind the Church

The missionaries, along with other foreign nationals, enjoyed a privileged status under the terms of treaties forced upon China by the foreign powers. They were in effect above Chinese law and enjoyed the backing of foreign consular officials and military power. Their missionary activity and their very presence in China was dependent upon foreign military power. As one Franciscan Sister, an American, wrote from a British steamer on the Chang Jiang, "Just a minute ago, while we were sitting on deck, two U.S.A. men of war passed us. We felt like swimming across and hugging them. All the cities of China are surrounded by warships of all nations, for protection. Without them, it would be impossible for foreigners to live in China."[2]

Although most American Catholic missionaries refused to use their privileged status under the unequal treaties, and although most had little or no contact with American, French, or Chinese government officials, there was no strong sentiment among them for the abolition of the unequal treaty system. In fact, American Dominicans sought to use both the American and the French consular officials to protect their missions in Fujian. The Vincentians in Jiangxi often called upon American officials to represent their interests and gunboats appeared on several occasions to rescue Dominicans, Maryknollers, and Franciscans.

As long as China was weak, the missionaries were able to enjoy their privileges. A strong, unified China, whatever its political persuasion, was not a comforting prospect for those who thought about the matter. In 1934, a Vincentian wrote from Jiangxi, "At times one wishes a Napoleon would arise and bring order out of chaos, but then the plight of the Church might be no better, for he might start a persecution in one form or another." Some years later another Vincentian, seeing the Nationalist government grow in strength and influence, considered it a new god worshiped by the Chinese. And the Jesuit planner George Dunne also fretted about the possibilities for an absolute state which he saw in the Nationalist Party.[3]

The Missionaries as Catalysts

Just as by their positive contributions in education and medicine the missionaries helped to set in motion and accelerate the process of modernization, so too by their rankling behavior they helped to set in motion and accelerate the process of antiforeignism. Both processes undermined the traditional Chinese society and, eventually, the foreign presence in China.

The educational work of the missionaries was a key factor in China's modernization. Missionary educators, especially Catholic clergy, contributed significantly to the spread of literacy among the peasantry, a class whose illiteracy had helped to keep it in bondage to the masters of the precapitalist social order. In the cities, Protestant missionaries instructed their pupils not only in the mysteries of the written word and technology but also in alternatives to China's social system. Thus although most of the Protestant missionaries wanted stability, not revolution or democracy, one of the Protestants' students, Sun Yixian (Sun Yat-sen), became the leader of the Chinese revolutionary movement of the late nineteenth and early twentieth century.[4]

The behavior of the missionaries often rankled the Chinese and engendered in them intense antiforeignism. When Chinese objected to the missionaries' meddling in the law courts, for example, a foreign consul was near at hand to threaten the use of force. When the Chinese fought against the meddling, foreign gunboats appeared to exact punitive damages. With those monies and alms collected abroad, the missioners built towering churches in the cities and large towns and an extensive network of institutions and residences. They also bought up land in the treaty ports and the countryside. In this fashion the Jesuits became the hated slumlords of Shanghai's Zhabei (Chapei) district.

The Economic Gulf Between Missionaries and Chinese

An economic chasm separated the missionaries from the Chinese and the missionaries were aware of the disparity. American Catholic missioners generally justified their relatively affluent life styles on the grounds that to live otherwise would endanger their health and the efficiency of their work and that "face" required them to adopt a wealthy style of life. One priest had another rationalization. "You know it's a fine thing," he wrote to Vincentian seminarians, "to preach mortification, sacrifices and all the virtues of our state, but it's another thing to put them into practice. In China a man's viewpoint on quite a few things change [sic]. Perhaps it's the climate that affects the missionaries. As it is said, why bring that up. We were talking about the dining room. What we need in the room would be a few traffic lights. Talk about service. We have four waiting on four priests and a half dozen more watching the show."[5]

The Vatican Deals with a Troubled Mission Field

Chinese nationalism and the widening gap between traditional and modern sectors of Chinese society were reaching crisis proportions for the Roman Church in China when conditions in Europe struck the Church an unexpected blow. The outbreak of World War I led to the desertion of hundreds of able-bodied European missionaries who went off to fight under their nations' standards. Throughout China, Roman Catholic missionary activity limped along through the agency of aged and invalid European priests, Sisters, and a small number of Chinese clergy.

Vatican officials saw in this setback an opportunity to compromise with the forces of both Chinese nationalism and modernization by redirecting mission activity in China. They now began to insist that foreign missionaries in China make substantial progress in developing a Chinese clergy and within a decade Roman authorities began to consecrate Chinese priests as bishops. The Vatican also began to promote the development of Chinese-style religious art and architecture in order to soften the foreign aspect of the Roman Church in China. Compromising with the forces of modernization was more difficult for the ancient institution which had just condemned religious "modernism." Vatican officials decided to sidestep Chinese demands for advanced education, an expensive proposition and one for which adequately trained personnel were in short supply. Instead, they would meet Chinese demands for English-medium instruction by sending Irish and American missionaries to fill in for the European missioners and conduct English-medium primary and secondary schools. The solution was not an ideal one, especially because the presence of more foreign missionaries could only intensify the Church's problems with Chinese nationalism.

American Catholic Missionaries Go to China

It was a propitious time for Rome to turn to the United States for Catholic missionaries. Catholics in the United States were caught in a double bind.

American Protestants, the dominant group, refused to accept them as truly American, while the Vatican treated them as second-class Catholics, infected by their Protestant environment. The institutional embodiment of the reaction to this dual rejection was the first American Catholic foreign missionary groups, the Catholic Foreign Mission Society of America, whose founders were a failed home missionary from North Carolina and an Irish-American sensitive to Roman disdain. In the mission areas, these two men and their followers believed they would achieve acceptance as Americans by the local people and as loyal co-workers by Roman authorities. "Oh you American youths," exclaimed Catholic Foreign Mission Society of America co-founder James A. Walsh, "what an opportunity is yours to lay out the ghosts of 'Americanism' and 'Modernism' that have floated from Europe over to the Far East!"[6]

For a very brief period after World War I when the first American Catholic missionaries began to go in groups to China, there was enthusiasm for mission work in China among some American Catholics. In addition to the Catholic Foreign Mission Society of America, one other group of American Catholic males, the American branch of the Passionist congregation, volunteered to do missionary work in China. That congregation's Roman headquarters urged its branches to expand into non-Christian lands and China seemed the most promising area to leaders of the American Passionist branch.

Under Vatican Pressure

Since two groups were not enough, the Vatican exerted pressure on other religious societies to send American members to China. Reluctantly, they complied. American Franciscans, Vincentians, Dominicans, Benedictines, and Jesuits went to China, many involuntarily or under false illusions. Some returned after only a short time in China. The more avid missioners convinced religious societies of women to work in China. Some were not above pressuring individual members of those societies into volunteering for work in China. Thus one Passionist missionary, Celestine Roddan, told a Daughter of Charity that it would be an abuse of grace if she didn't volunteer. When a priest confessor concurred, the Sister volunteered.[7]

Zeal for the China missions or for foreign missions in general was not a characteristic of the American Catholic clergy or members of religious societies during the interwar period. A study of 7500 people who entered the seminary or convent between 1919 and 1929 indicated that only five percent of the men and five percent of the women gave "foreign missions" as their strongest vocational motive. Among both men and women, "foreign missions" ranked ninth on a list of vocational motives, a list topped by "personal salvation."[8]

During this period domestic operations preoccupied the American Catholic clergy and most religious communities. When there was interest in foreign missionary work, other areas began to draw interest away from China. By 1940, for example, less than one percent of American Catholic Sisters were working in the foreign missions, and of those only one-fourth, 291, were working in China.[9]

Nor was the Catholic community at large enthusiastic about foreign missions. The editor of *Catholic Missions* estimated in 1925 that at least two-thirds of America's 18,000,000 Catholics were unconcerned about the missions. He further estimated that 3,200,000 gave something for their support and a bare 10,000 worked for them.[10]

Propelled by the Young

Most of the enthusiasm and support for the American Catholic foreign mission efforts came from the young.[11] Mission organization publicists, with varying success, cultivated anti-Protestantism, American nationalism, insecurity, and compassion to engender this zeal in youthful co-religionists.[12]

The main mission-oriented organization for young Catholics and the most vital missionary support organization in American Catholicism was the Catholic Students Mission Crusade. Founded in 1918 by two seminarians, it had grown to 500,000 members by 1933 and two years later one writer termed it America's most powerful Catholic youth movement.[13]

Enthusiasm for the missions tapered off after 1935. John LaFarge, S.J., reported to his Roman superior that troubled conditions in mission lands, domestic problems, deepening isolationist spirit, and "a growing distaste for insecurity and adventure, coupled with the wearing off of the novelty of the foreign mission field" were eroding interest in the missions. "The Catholic Students Mission Crusade which started off as such a powerful auxiliary to the missions," LaFarge commented, "has been obliged to take up a variety of home interests—social, religious, etc.,—to keep up interest and obtain members.[14]

A Peripheral but Important Role at Home

Small and peripheral as they were, the American Catholic missions to China were important in the history of the Roman Catholic Church in the United States, making vital contributions to the sociopsychological dimension of the American Catholic community and to the institutional stability of the Church in America. The American Church had entered the twentieth century under the cloud of the "Americanism" heresy and a perennial nativistic anti-Catholicism. The "modernism" heresy scare dampened the church's spirit still further. World War I shut off immigration and initiated the American government's antihyphenation campaign, which attacked large segments of the Church's membership. In the following decade a "truly alarming" defection of members plagued it.[15]

During the 1930s, the economic depression stunned the church and its membership stagnated. Through most of this period, the China missions were rallying points for the fervent, especially the impressionable young. They were all the more effective as rallying points because mission publicists habitually played down losses and frustrations in the work and made the missions seem more successful than they really were. James E. Walsh was even able to draw some comfort for anxious American Catholics from the murder of Fr. Gerard Donovan by Manchurian bandits. Donovan's death, he proclaimed, answered the old doubts about the apostolic zeal of individual American priests. Walsh summed up his view of the "martyr's" role as an instrument in God's hand: "Maryknoll is complete and America is apostolic."[16]

The China missions also had an important institutional role as safety valves for the Catholic Church in the United States. When the first band of missionaries went to China in 1918, they were leaving behind a church that was no longer stimulated by the challenge of immigration and whose basic organizational work had been accomplished at the diocesan and parish levels. In several seaboard dioceses there was not enough room for more priests, and aspirants to the priesthood were being turned away from the seminary doors. In the Midwest, there was no shortage of Sisters and by the mid-thirties, according to one estimate, one of every eight eligible American Catholic girls was entering the convent. In the East, the personnel needs of the parochial schools kept a surplus of Sisters from developing. As might be expected, a sample of China mission veterans indicated that the men's religious communities were drawing heavily from the eastern United States for their China missionaries, while midwestern religious communities of women supplied the most Sisters to the China missions.[17]

By drawing so many priests from the eastern United States and Sisters from the Midwest, the China missions served two functions. First, they relieved the pressure of a surplus of religious aspirants. The church was thus able to maintain its image as an organization with room for new workers and thereby provide against the possibility that most potential aspirants would not even bother to inquire about church employment. Otherwise, once diverted, there could be no guarantee that the stream of recruits would flow churchward again. Second, the China missions were outlets and dumping grounds for enthusiasts, mavericks, and misfits. But these were the very sort of personnel the church needed to avoid slipping from stability into self-complacent torpor, irrelevancy, and decline. When such persons went to China, they left behind a less vital corps to manage the Church.

The Missionary Business

When the Americans arrived in China they found it an arena of contention among the various religious groups. Even within the groups, national branches squabbled with one another. The divisiveness which sapped the energies of the missionaries was rooted in institutional ambition and nationalism. The Americans could not escape the turmoil because the European missionary societies generally resisted the loss of mission territory which justified the societies' existence and was endowed with indemnity monies. Even when they did turn over territory, the European societies often sought to keep control of most or all of the wealth attached to each territory. This led to contention and Vatican intervention. The Vatican's solution was to force the Europeans to give up part of their ecclesiastical territory to the Americans while allowing them to retain most of the treasure for use in their shrunken territories.

The American missionaries also struggled with Chinese churchmen over financial matters. In Jiangxi the American Vincentians sought to keep the better mission stations for their own use and were successful in preventing the establishment of an independent mission run by the Chinese clergy. In Guangdong, the Maryknollers adopted a policy which excluded Chinese clergy from their Jiangmen mission territory for many years. They were thus able to retain work for themselves and to promote their society as one which needed more American recruits and financial support.

In the United States, competition among the various mission groups for personnel and alms was strenuous. In their fundraising they also competed with the National Society for the Propagation of the Faith and with local pastors and bishops who wanted the money of American Catholics for themselves and their work. An American Dominican provincial superior was moved to write, "The Propagation of the Faith is trying to hog everything and I fear we shall have difficulty in raising funds for our Missions in the future."[18]

Consciousness of this competitive, entrepreneurial dimension of missionary work occasionally appeared in the missionary ranks. Vincentian Father James J. Corbett, commenting on his hard work as agent for his congregation's Ganzhou vicariate apostolic and the fact that by taking risks he had gotten a better currency exchange rate than the agents of the other ten Vincentian-managed vicariates apostolic, crowed, "We are establishing mission traditions of our own. We are breaking some old ones but we are getting there—I mean progressing despite the fact that the world grinned when America entered the foreign mission business (?). Like many things else the Yankees have injected a little of the new much to the benefit of the human race."[19]

The chief concern of the American Catholic missionaries was maintaining the allegiance of Chinese Catholics, not proselytizing non-Christians. Except for the Maryknoller F.X. Ford in the Mei Xian vicariate, the Americans made no significant departures from generally established mission methods. Although often above average in pastoral effectiveness, they were not outstanding proselytizers. In Guangdong, Fujian, Hunan, and Manchuria, their failure as proselytizers was pronounced. Much of the growth of their missions, in fact, came from natural increase and from orphanages.

Internal Deficiencies

Certainly, antiforeignism and troubled political conditions hindered the work of the American Catholic missionaries. Moreover, personal and institutional factors further compromised their activities. The missionaries generally failed to learn Chinese well. Most of their groups suffered from hidebound traditionalism and a general spirit of clericalism. There was both an institutional and a personal interest in the perpetuation of the mission work at the expense of the development of a Chinese clergy and active laity. These were important reasons for the failure of the American Catholic missions. The fundamental weakness, which they shared with their European counterparts, was the failure to present the Chinese with a socially viable way of life that was simultaneously acceptable to the Church and to the Chinese people as a whole. Instead they urged upon the Chinese the Roman Catholic way of life, the greater part of which, noted the influential Jesuit social activist John LaFarge in the 1940s, was "consumed with individual religious practice." The Maryknoll Father John J. Considine added that not only were catechisms "devoted almost exclusively" to individual religious practice but also "that the missioner who goes abroad continues this policy of making strong individual Catholics." Considine stressed that the Catholic missionary, American included, "seldom emphasizes cooperation in public affairs, or . . . cooperation among peoples on the basis of open advocacy of Catholic teaching, any more than does the priest at home. . . . Cooperation between peoples . . . means little to the individual Catholic teacher, either in Asia or in America."[20]

Positive Accomplishments

Although they did and said nothing deliberately to undermine the status quo in China, the American Catholic missionaries worked hard on behalf of tens of thousands of individual Chinese and thus, ultimately, in behalf of the new Chinese society struggling to be born around them. By 1940, four of eighteen American Catholic missions had hospitals and eight had orphanages. There were 270 grammar schools, 600 rudimentary schools, and five high schools.[21]

Some schools would soon pass from the scene as the Chinese government built alternatives; others would live on as outposts of literacy in the struggle to demystify the written word. Furthermore, American Catholic missionaries, who over the years had functioned as paramedical workers and as nurses in rural areas and towns, cared for thousands of soldiers and civilians wounded by the Japanese. As they had during the warlord era, the missionaries threw open their compounds to refugees and shared their own food with them. Some missionaries even cooperated with the Chinese resistance forces by gathering and transmitting intelligence for them and by sharing food and medicine with them.

The Effect of a Dozen Years of War

Although the forces of disintegration had been taking their toll on the Catholic Church in China for some years, World War II was the immediate cause of the collapse of the Roman Catholic missionary effort in China. The war scattered Catholic communities and left church property extensively damaged or destroyed. At the time of the attack on Pearl Harbor there were 671 American Catholic missionaries in China.[22] The Japanese interned many of them and repatriated some. Most of them left the country before 1945. Missionaries able to remain at their posts often became impoverished and were forced to suspend their church work. By 1945 the Catholic Church in China was a battered shell.

After World War II, there was a brief lull in China before the outbreak of a terrible civil war between Nationalists and Communists. Missionaries returned to their old districts to find missions destroyed by Japanese, American, or Chinese bombs and found themselves in a crossfire between the combatants. Mission activity declined and so did the fortunes of the Catholic Church. Although the Vatican pressed ahead with the establishment of a Chinese hierarchy, the Chinese clergy displayed an antiforeignism that demoralized some of the foreign missionaries and gave them added reason to leave the war-torn land against the Vatican's explicit wishes.

The end of the Chinese civil war temporarily halted the physical destruction suffered by the Catholic Church and set the stage for a massive confrontation between the Church and the new Communist regime. The land reform program stripped the Church of much of its rural property, including churches. The outbreak of the Korean War and Chinese participation against the United States in the northern half of the Korean peninsula embittered the Chinese Communists against a Church openly identified with foreign imperialism and anti-Communism and staffed in part by Americans who had recently served with American military and intelligence units in China.

Although it was successful in expelling the foreign missionaries, developing an acquiescent group of Chinese Catholic clergy, and accelerating the decline in the number of active Chinese Catholics, the Communist regime was not able to eliminate Catholicism in China. Indeed, as its fourth decade in power began, the regime invited French Jesuit professors of medicine to return to teach at Aurora University in Shanghai.[23] Two centuries before, the Qing had harbored Jesuit scholars at the Imperial Court while they struggled to eliminate Christianity, a doctrine which Qing statesmen saw as an ideological alternative to Confucianism. Conceivably, Chinese Communist statesmen, intent on the rapid modernization of China, were being as flexible as Qing statesmen. Perhaps they sought to draw the French to their side in China's continuing war of nerves with Russia. Or perhaps the Vatican's diplomatic flexibility in its "opening to the left" and the growing identification of the Church with revolutionary social movements in Latin America might have altered the Chinese Communist leadership's perception of Roman Catholicism. If that were the case, then some American Catholic missionaries prominent in Latin American political struggles for a new social order, most notably Maryknoll priests and Sisters, played a role in convincing the Chinese to invite the Jesuits back to China.

Notes

Abbreviations Used in Notes

ASC	Archives, Adorers of the Blood of Christ, Ruma, Ill.
CMJ	Archives, Congregation of the Mission, St. John's University, Jamaica, New York.
CMStL	Archives, Congregation of the Mission, St. Louis, Mo.
CPUC	Archives, Congregation of the Passion, St. Michael's Monastery, Union City, N. J.
FSPA	Archives, Franciscan Sisters of Perpetual Adoration, La Crosse, Wisc.
GMD	Gaozhou Mission Diary
LMD	Luoding Mission Diary
MM	Archives, Catholic Foreign Mission Society of America, Maryknoll, N.Y.
OFMStL	Archives, Order of Friars Minor, St. Louis, Mo.
OPDC	Archives, Order of Preachers, Washington, D. C.
SJLG	Archives, Society of Jesus, California province, Los Gatos, Cal.
SPSM	Archives, Sisters of Providence, St. Mary's of the Woods, Ind.
USNA/RG59	United States, Department of State, Decimal File, Record Group 59, National Archives, Washington, D.C.
WL	*Woodstock Letters.*
WMD	Wuzhou Mission Diary

Complete publishing information can be found in the Select Bibliography following the Notes.

Preface

1. Joseph L. Grabill, "The 'Invisible' Missionary: A Study in American Foreign Relations," *Journal of Church and State* 14:1 (Winter 1972): 92-105. Grabill deplores the neglect of American Protestant missionaries in standard American diplomatic history books. He completely ignores American Catholic missionaries.

2. John K. Fairbank, ed., *The Missionary Enterprise in China and America* (Cambridge: Harvard University Press, 1974).

3. Frederick B. Hoyt, "Protection Implies Intervention: The U.S. Catholic Mission at Kanchow," *The Historian* 38 (August 1976); Nancy B. Tucker, "An Unlikely Peace: American Missionaries and the Chinese Communists," *Pacific Historical Review* 45:1 (Feb. 1976): 97-116.

Introduction

1. Yang, p.3.

2. Hazelrigg, argues persuasively on the basis of his study of the Italian population that alienation from the Church affected all Italian social strata.

3. Latourette, pp. 46-198, and Cary-Elwes, passim, are, except where noted, the narrative sources of the foregoing account. The interpretation is mine.

Chapter 1

1. Immanuel C.Y. Hsü, p. 225.

2. Colombel, p. 912. See also pp. 237, 241, 424, 411; La Serviere, p. 24; Colombel, pp. 72, 73, 141-43, 377-79, 381. La Serviere's work is that of a court historian and should be read as such.

3. La Serviere, p. 24, notes that in 1840 a Vincentian missionary, Père Lavaissiere, had undertaken to impose a discipline on the virgins of the Jiangnan mission. He was not successful.

4. Colombel, p. 323; La Serviere, pp. 98 ff.

5. Colombel, pp. 553-54.

6. Teng, pp. 202-5; Jen, pp. 127, 414.

7. Colombel, p. 918.

8. Ibid., p. 912.

9. Francis X. Ford, "Substituting for a Month," Xingning [Hingming], 21 May 1934, MM.

10. Crapez, pp. 15, 53-54.

11. Latourette, pp. 329, 330, 351, 356, 362.

12. William L. Hornsby, S.J., letter from Macao, 14 Oct. 1892, in *WL*, 22:1 (1893): 21-22.

13. Latourette, p. 549; J.A. Gately, C.M., to Crusaders, Xinfeng, Jiangxi, 19 Nov. 1929, CMJ.

14. Hinton, pp. 61-62.

15. Paul Curran, O.P., to Fr. Meagher, O.P., Fuzhou, Fujian, 23 Jan. 1925, OPDC.

16. Père Vinchon, S.J., to Mr. Weber, S.J., in *WL* 20:3 (1891).

17. *WL* 33:1 (1904): 122; Laurence J. Kenney, S.J., "Early American Missionaries," *WL* 83:2 (May 1954): 202-3.

18. Wlodimir Ledochowski, General of the Society of Jesus, to all the provincials [provincial superiors] of the American Assistancy, Rome 9 May 1935, *WL* 66:1 (1937): 87-92.

19. *Atlas Hierarchicus*, p. 14; Lazaristes du Peit'ang (Peiping), passim.

20. S. Espelage, O.F.M., to Fr. Noel, O.F.M., Wuchang, 11 and 12 Dec. 1921, OFMStL.

Chapter 2

1. Paul A. Varg, *Missionaries, Chinese, and Diplomats* (Princeton: Princeton University Press, 1956), pp. 52-67.

2. Mark Stolarik, "Lay Initiative in America-Slovak Parishes: 1880-1930," *Records of the American Catholic Historical Society of Philadelphia* 83:3-4 (Sept.-Dec. 1972): 151-58; William Galush, "The Polish National Catholic Church: A Survey of Its Origins, Development and Missions," ibid., pp. 131-49.

3. Michael V. Gannon, "Before and After Modernism: The Intellectual Isolation of the American Priest," in John Tracy Ellis, ed., *The Catholic Priest in the United States: Historical Investigations* (Collegeville, Minn., 1971), pp. 293-383; for the tensions between diocesan and religious order clergy, John P. Marschall's essay, "Diocesan and Religious Clergy: The History of a Relationship, 1789-1969," ibid., pp. 385-421, is a fine overview.

4. Gleason, passim.

5. An impressive criticism of the Irish-Liberal claim that the immigrants and their children had clung to Catholicism is made by Moore.

6. *Official Catholic Directory*; Andrew Sinclair, *The Era of Excess* (New York: Harper, 1964), p. 64.

7. "Our Advance in China," *Catholic Missions* 8 (March 1914): 69.

8. "Why All For China?" *Catholic Missions* 12 (May 1918): 119.

9. *America* 7 (26 July 1919): 271-72; ibid. 5 (2 Sept. 1911): 490. A bleaker view was expressed in *Catholic Missions* 9 (March 1915): 71. The theme of China as a locus of Catholic-Protestant competition continued for years. Catholic publicists depicted Protestantism as facilitating the rise and spread of Chinese Communism. *America* 69 (5 Aug. 1933): 412-13; Patrick Ward, "China, Greatest of Problems," *Commonweal* 3 (25 Nov. 1925): 71-73; King, pp. 85-87; "A Returned Missionary," "Crisis in the East," *The Sign* 17 (April 1938): 543-44.

10. Latourette, p. 717. For an account of American Catholic donations to the worldwide mission effort fostered by the Society for the Propagation of the Faith in the years prior to 1922, see Hickey, pp. 116-17; 121-26. An overview of the resurgence of the Catholic missions is given by Hickey, pp. 130-53.

11. Latourette, p. 706.

12. USNA/RG 59, 393.116/163; /163½; /164; /164½; /167; /170; /171; /172; /173;/175;/177;/178;/182;/182½;/189.

13. Keller and Berger, p. 34; Kitner; Lane; J. A. Walsh to J.E.W., 6 Sept. 1927, MM.

14. Superior General to Fr. Finney, Rome, 23 Aug. 1922; Fr. Misner, C.M., to Fr. Barr, C.M., San Francisco, 26 May 1926, CMStL.

15. Decrees, General Chapter, Sec. 111, No. 3; Province of St. Paul of the Cross, 20th Provincial Chapter, 20-28 Aug. 1920; Alfred Cagney, C.P., to V. Rev. Justin Carey, C.P., Rome, 1 Feb. 1921, 1 Apr. 1921, 19 May 1921, 7 Aug. 1921, and 4 Sept. 1921; Maguire, p. 12.

16. S. Espelage, O.F.M., to V. Rev. Rudolf Bonner, Wuchang, 25 Feb. 1921; S. Espelage to Fr. Noel, O.F.M., Wuchang, 11 and 12 Dec. 1921; V. Rev. Seraphin [Ainsino?], Minister General, to V. Reverend Fathers Provincial (U.S.A.), Rome, 14 July 1920, OFMStL.

17. V. Rev. Seraphin, Minister General, to V. Rev. Fathers Provincial (U.S.A.), Rome, 14 July 1920, OFMStL.

18. Habig, *Journeyings*, p. 315; Freundt, pp. 59-79.

19. Bro. Alfred Sullivan, O.P., "The American Dominican Territory in China," *Dominicana* 8:2 (Sept. 1923): 6; Reilly, pp. 331-43, esp. pp. 331-34. Reilly claims that Propaganda Fide conceded the mission to St. Joseph Province in 1918. The earliest date for the concession that I could find in the archival material indicates late 1923 as the official date, but there are indications of previous informal planning. Reilly's date for the assignment of the mission by Propaganda Fide is in harmony with the review of China mission needs being conducted by that office about that time. The four-year delay in even inspecting the mission territory is consonant with the intense American Dominican emphasis on domestic expansion at that time.

20. P. Curran, O.P., to V. Rev. L.F. Kearney, O.P., Fuzhou, 30 Oct. 1923, OPDC.

21. "Excerpts from the Chronicle of the Catholic University of Peking," *Fu Jen Magazine* 4 (Oct. 1935): 154-55.

22. Ralph J. Deward, S.J., "China's Martyr of Charity," *China Letter*, no. 27 (Apr. 1938): 1; Lu Pahang to Fr. Provincial (Cal. Province), S.S. *President Pierce*, 11 Aug. 1926, SJLG.

23. Msgr. Howard P. Lawton, interview with the author, Philadelphia, 1 July 1971.

24. Caspar Conley, C.P., to Fr. Provincial, Yuanling, Hunan, 28 Oct. 1928, CPUC; Rev. Francis Moehringer, C.M., to George Moehringer, C.M., Longnan, Jiangxi, 10 Oct. 1924, CMJ; Fr. [McHale?], C.M., to Fr. E.T. Sheehan, C.M., n.p., 20 Oct. 1928, CMStL.

25. Edward T. Sheehan, C.M., to V. Rev. William P. Barr, C.M., Boyang, Jiangxi, 10 Aug. 1928, CMStL; Z.J. Maher to Fr. L.F. McGreel, n.p., 15 May 1934, SJLG (With this letter Maher announced that henceforth the California Province would be sending "ordinary" men to China.); J.E.W. to J.A. Walsh, Guangdong, 4 Apr. 1926; Xiachuan, 20 Apr. 1926; Jiangmen, 30 June 1926, MM.

26. B.C. Werner to R. Meagher, Washington, D.C., 9 May [1924?]; P. Curran, O.P., to R. Meagher, Nandai, 24 Dec. 1924; Reilly, p. 36; Curran to Meagher, Jian'ou, 19 May 1926 and 13 Apr. 1926; Thomas H. Sullivan, O.P., to Meagher, [Jian'ou?], 8 Nov. 1926; Curran to Meagher, Jian'ou, 9 Sept. 1925; anon., ms. history of Jian'ou mission (n.d., n.p.), p. 1, OPDC; author's survey, summer 1970; Fr. Misner, C.M., to Fr. Flavin, C.M., Yujiang, Jiangxi, 26 Feb. 1936, CMStL.

27. Celestine Roddan to Fr. Grennan, Zhijiang, 10 July, 1922, CPUC.

28. Rev. Gerald Pope, S.J., interview with author, Los Altos, Cal., 6 Sept. 1971; John F. Magner, S.J., conversations with the author, Los Gatos, Cal., 26 Aug., 2 Sept. 1971; L.F. McGreal, S.J., to Fr. Provincial, Shanghai, 2 May 1933; Ralph Deward, S.J., to Fr. Provincial, Jiangsu, 27 Apr. 1935. Deward observed in that letter, "Our formative years are difficult but doubly so in China. I grant that there are men of the [George] Dunne and [Paul] O'Brien type that can make it, but for the ordinary man, its [sic] almost beyond his powers. Much depends upon the character of a man and upon his ability. If one is talented, the strain is only ½ fold. But even the talented go down. Look at Mr. [Francis] Rouleau, bright man that he is, [he] has felt the strain almost from the beginning and has cracked periodically."

29. Fr. Misner, C.M., to Fr. Flavin, C.M., Jiujiang, Jiangxi, 13 Nov. 1934, CMStL.

30. J.P. Mc Cormack to J.A. Walsh, Fushun, 6 Aug. 1930, MM.

31. Fr. Misner, C.M., to Fr. Barr, C.M., San Francisco, 26 May 1926, CMStL.

32. J.F. Kearney, S.J., to Z.J. Maher, S.J., Shanghai, 25 Aug. 1934, SJLG.

33. Sr. M. Gratia to Rev. Mother M. Raphael, Kaifeng, 22 May 1933, SPSM.

34. Sr. M. Gratia to Rev. Mother M. Raphael, Kaifeng, 24 Jan. 1938, SPSM.

35. Gutteres, p. 5; Annals, Bin Xian, 16 Sept. 1935, ASC.

36. Paul Ubinger, C.P., to Fr. Provincial, Yuanling, 16 Nov. 1924, CPUC; Timothy McDermott, C.P., to Rev. Stanislaus Grennan, C.P., Zhijiang, Hunan, 19 Sept. 1922, CPUC.
37. Sr. Jeanne Marie pp. 93, 17, 91, 97, 105; Sheridan, p. 4; J.E.W. to J.A. Walsh, Baiqi, 3 March 1927, MM.
38. Unsigned letter, 1946, in Maryknoll Sisters' Mission Research Library, Rogers College, Maryknoll, N.Y.
39. Ralph Townsend, *Ways That Are Dark: The Truth About China* (New York: G.P. Putnam's, 1933), pp. 137-9.
40. Timothy McDermott, C.P., to Fr. Master Grennan, 19 Sept. 1922, Zhijiang, Hunan, CPUC.
41. Ambrose Pinger, O.F.M., to Fr. Provincial, Zhoucun, 4 March 1936, OFMStL.

Chapter 3
1. F.X. Ford to Maryknollers, Yangjiang, 6 Apr. 1921, MM.
2. F.X. Ford, "Substituting for a Month," Xingming, 21 May 1934, MM.
3. Erbashi Mission Diarist, Erbashi Mission Diary, 16 June 1927; A. Jacques, M.M., to Maryknoll Erbashi, n.d. [received at Maryknoll, 7 March 1930]; A. Jacques, M.M., to ————, Erbashi, 19 March 1930, MM.
4. Luoding Mission Diarist, LMD, 28 Dec. 1919 to Jan. 1920, p. 63, MM; Fr. O'Shea to Brother Killoren, Pingnan, 1 May 1922, MM.
5. Lazaristes de Peit'ang, passim.
6. Leon Cahill to Vincentian students, Ganzhou, 26 Dec. 1922, CMJ; Luoding Mission Diarist, LMD, 10 March 1922, MM; Lazaristes de Peit'ang, passim.
7. Luoding Mission Diarist [J.E.W.], LMD, 15-30 Aug. 1920, MM.
8. From an obituary for Monsignor Sylvester Espelage, O.F.M., *Franciscans in China* 13 (1940): 103-7; Lazaristes de Peit'ang, passim.
9. Interview with Fr. John Tu, Taizhong, 24 Sept. 1971; interview with Fr. Protase Pai, Taizhong, 24 Sept. 1971.
10. Quentin Olwell, C.P., in an interview in Union City, N.J., 24 Nov. 1970, stressed the barrier of celibacy to the development of a Chinese priest class. In an interview at Taizhong, Taiwan (23 Sept. 1971) Albert V. Fedders, a former Maryknoll seminary teacher in South China, stressed the barriers posed by an extremely long training period and a Western-oriented curriculum in which the Latin language was overemphasized to prove to the bishops and to the Vatican that the Maryknollers were running a seminary as good as any seminary anywhere. "*Relatio Extraordinaria Vicariatus* Kongmoon" (June 1927, MM) bears out Fedders' description of the substance and length of the program. The eight- or nine-year program of the Maryknoll preparatory seminary that opened at Jiangmen in 1925 with six students was typical. It included two years of Chinese upper elementary school education followed by six years of secondary schooling, including study of ancient and modern Chinese, religion, science, math, English, and Latin. Latin was taught the full eight or nine years with instruction given in Latin grammar and the works of secular and religious authors such as Nepos, Caesar, Cicero, Vergil, Tacitus, and Horace. After finishing the courses at the seminary, which was staffed by an American priest and two Chinese laymen, aspirants to the priesthood had six to eight more years of training in western scholastic philosophy and theology.
11. Quentin Olwell, C.P., in an interview with the author, Union City, N.J., 24 Nov. 1971.

12. Gaozhou Mission Diarist [O'Shea], GMD, 5 March 1921, pp. 252-3, MM.

13. P. Curran to Fr. Kearney, Jian'ou, 4 Sept. 1924, OPDC; McDermott to Grennan, Zhijiang, 19 Sept. 1922, CPUC; C. Roddan to Grennan, Yuanling, 10 June 1922; V. Rev. Fr. Provincial to the Fathers and Brothers in China, [Union City, N.J.?], 20 May 1926, CPUC.

14. "China Calls," *The Sign* (Nov. 1921): 23.

15. James J. Corbett, C.M., to Vincentian Novices, Ganzhou, Nov. 1924, CMJ.

16. Donovan, p. 69; Maguire, p. 17; Bauer, p. 94.

17. [W. J. Downs], "Enforced Silent Night: A Historical Record of the Kaying Diocese, 1845–1961" (unpublished manuscript, 1962), pp. 19, 56, MM.

18. F.J. Stauble, C.M., to "Oaky," C.M., Ganzhou, 18 Apr. 1926, CMJ.

19. Raphael Vance to Fr. Provincial, Baojing, 23 Aug. 1923, 21 Oct. 1924, CPUC.

20. Maoming Mission Diarist [Meyer], Maoming Mission Diary, 1-23 Apr. 1922, MM.

21. Wuzhou Mission Diarist [Dietz?], WMD, 2 Jan. 1921, p. 18, MM; [B. F. Meyer?], Dongzhen, 1 Aug. 1920, *Maryknoll Mission Letters* I, 232.

22. B.F. Meyer to Fr. Superior, Dongzhen, 13 Jan. 1920, MM.

23. Luoding Mission Diarist, LMD, 15–30 Aug. 1920, p. 32, MM. Though lengthier than some, the ninety-day-long catechumenates conducted by the Passionists were typical in their format. According to Bp. Cuthbert O'Gara's "Quinquennial Report, Diocese of Yuanling, 1951," pp. 36-37 (CPUC), a typical day was as follows:

a.m.			p.m.	
6:00	Rise		1:15	Class in prayers, the meaning of the prayers by the catechist
6:30	Holy Mass and Morning Prayers			
7:15	Memorize catechism lesson of preceding day		2:15	Memorize the prayers
			3:15	Stories from the Old and New Testaments linked to the catechism lesson of the day or to a feast
8:15	Breakfast			
9:00	Class in the Chinese characters of the catechism lesson, the meaning of each phrase			
			4:15	Recreation
10:00	Memorize the characters		5:00	Supper
11:00	Explanation of the catechism by the missionary or a teaching Sister		6:00	Evening prayers
12:00	Noon meal			

For working men who cannot come to classes during the day a different program is followed. They attend evening classes.

p.m.			a.m.	
6:00	Evening prayers		6:00	Rise
6:30	Explanation of the doctrine of the catechism lesson by the missionary		6:30	Holy Mass and morning prayers
			7:15	Memorize catechism
7:15	Word-by-word explanation of the characters by the missionary		8:15	Breakfast
8:00	Bible history story			
8:30	Memory work			

24. Paul Ubinger to Grennan, Chenxi, 10 July 1923; Paul Ubinger to Fr. Provincial, Yuanling, 16 Nov. 1924, CPUC.

25. J.J. Corbett, to Richard A. Loeffler, n.C.M., Ganzhou, 16 Oct. 1928, CMJ.

26. Leon Cahill to Vincentian students, Ganzhou, 26 Dec. 1922, CMJ; James J. Corbett, C.M., to President, CSMC, C.M. Unit, Germantown, Pa., Ganzhou, 16 May 1926, CMJ.

27. J.E.W. to Fr. Superior, Gaungzhou, n.d. [received at Maryknoll 31 Dec. 1918], MM.

28. T. Price to Fr. General, Yangjiang, 12 March 1919, MM.

29. Bauer, p. 105.

30. Gaozhou Mission Diarist [O'Shea], GMD, 4 Dec. 1919, pp. 30–31, 7 Jan. 1921, pp. 239–43, MM.

31. J.J. Corbett to Richard A. Loeffler, n.C.M., Ganzhou, 16 Oct. 1928, CMJ; Wuzhou Mission Diarist, WMD, Nov. 1920, p. 3, MM; J.E.W. to J.A. Walsh, Shanghai, 8 June 1924, MM.

32. Gaozhou Mission Diarist [O'Shea], GMD, 7 Jan. 1921, pp. 239–43, MM.

33. F.X. Ford, untitled article received at Maryknoll, 20 Apr. 1921, MM.

34. Gaozhou Mission Diarist [O'Shea], GMD, 5 March 1921, pp. 254–55, MM.

35. Wuzhou Mission Diarist, WMD, 20–27 June 1921, pp. 57–65, MM; Gaozhou Mission Diarist, GMD, late June 1921 to 5 July 1921, pp. 111 ff., MM; Fr. Crossley to Catholic Students Mission Crusade Unit, St. Joseph's College, Princeton, N.J., Nananfu, 16 Jan. 1925, CMJ.

36. Dominic Langenbacher, C.P., "The Arrival of the Passionists," in *Relacion Del Vicariato De Hunan Septentrional (China)*, CPUC; American Consul, Changsha, 12 Jan. 1924, No. 452, 393.1163 Am3/12, USNA/RG59.

37. American Vice-Consul, Changsha [Meinhardt], to Gen. Zhao Hengdi, 11 Jan. 1924, 393.1163 Am3/12 [enclosure], USNA/RG59. The American minister to China also lodged a vigorous protest. See Flavian Mullins to Fr. Provincial, Xupu, 29 Feb. 1924; Flavian Mullins to Consultor, Xupu, 9 Apr. 1925, CPUC; American Consul, Changsha, to the Secretary of State, 13 Apr. 1925, 393.1163 Am3/15, USNA/RG59.

38. American Consul General, Wuhan, to the Secretary of State, No. 896, 16 Dec. 1924, 393.116/337, USNA/RG59; William Westhoven, C.P., p. 57; Maguire, pp. 38, 65.

39. Curran to Meagher, Jian'ou, 9 Sept. 1925, OPDC.

40. D. Langenbacher to Fr. Provincial, Yuanling, 24 Nov. 1924, CPUC.

41. [Fr. O'Shea], via Fr. Burke of the National Catholic Welfare Conference, to Mr. Lockhart of the Department of State, 21 March 1925, MM.

42. J.E.W. to J.A. Walsh, Hong Kong, 11 July 1925, MM; J.E.W. to J.A. Walsh, Hong Kong, 24 Aug. 1925; J.E.W. to J.A. Walsh, Jiangmen, 24 Oct. 1925, MM; J.E.W. to J.A. Walsh, Hong Kong, 11 July 1925, MM.

Chapter 4

1. J.E.W. to J.A. Walsh, Jiangmen, 1 June 1927, MM.

2. Xiachuan Island Diarist [Burns], Xiachuan Island Diary, Nov. 1926 to Feb. 1927, p. 5; 2 June 1927, p. 11; 6 Jan. 1927, p. 4. The Purgatorial and Aid Societies also had a share in two of the local loan societies. See ibid., 20 Feb. 1927, p. 5.

3. Ibid., 2 June 1927, p. 11; Feb. 1927, pp. 4–5.

4. Ibid., Feb. 1927, p. 5.

5. American Consul, Fuzhou (Burke) to Secretary of State, 24 Dec. 1931, 393.1163/540, USNA/RG59.

6. Raphael L. McDonald, O.F.M., "Prefecture Apostolic of Shasi" (M.A. thesis, St. Bonaventure University, 1945), pp. 12–15.

7. Gutteres, pp. 26–27; "Chronology," SPSM.

8. J.A. O'Shea, C.M. to confrere [Ganzhou?], 12 Nov. 1926, CMJ; J.J. Corbett, C.M., to Vincentian Novices, Ganzhou, 22 Nov. 1926, CMJ; J.S. Gately, C.M., to Crusaders, Xinfeng, 13 July 1929, CMJ; Wm. J. McClimont, S.M., to Donald G. Knox, Ganzhou, 20 Dec. 1926, CMJ.

9. Ibid.; Rev. Francis Moehringer, C.M., to George [Moehringer?], Longnan, 20 Jan. 1927, CMJ.

10. Ibid.; Wm. J. McClimont, S.M., to Donald G. Knox, Ganzhou, 20 Dec. 1926, CMJ.

11. Frank [Stauble?] to Family, Longnan, 17 Dec. 1926; Wm. J. McClimont to Crusaders, Ganzhou, 22 Apr. 1927, CMJ.

12. Maguire, pp. 65, 66, 79, 85; Cuthbert O'Gara, C.P., to Rt. Rev. Dominic Langenbacher, C.P., Yuanling, 14 Jan. 1927, 15 Jan. 1927, 18 Jan. 1927, and 24 Jan. 1927, CPUC.

13. C. O'Gara, C.P., to D. Langenbacher, Yuanling, 24 Jan. 1927, CPUC.

14. R. Meagher to E. Hughes, New York City, 7 Oct. 1927, OPDC; American Consul, Fuzhou (Burke) to Secretary of State, 24 Dec. 1931, 393.1163/540, USNA/RG59.

15. D. Langenbacher to Fr. Provincial, Zhijiang, 31 Jan. 1927, CPUC; Westhoven, pp. 56–57; Anthony Maloney, C.P., "A Heroine of 1927," in *The Sign*, eds., *Eyes East*, pp. 45–46; Sisters of St. Joseph of Baden, Pa., *China*, vol. 1, *History*, passim; Maguire, pp. 103–7; Gutteres, pp. 26–27.

16. "Chronology," SPSM; B.C. Werner to T.S. McDermott, O.P., China, 31 Aug. 1944, OPDC.

17. Meagher to J.J. Burke, C.S.P., [New York?], 12 Sept. 1928, OPDC; P. Curran to R. Meagher, Jian'ou, 18 Oct. 1928, OPDC.

18. American Consul General (Huston) to Secretary of State, 30 Nov. 1927, 393.1163 Am3/42, USNA/RG59; Brother Michael to J.A. Walsh, Jiangmen, 23 Nov. 1927, MM; J.E.W. to J.A. Walsh, Jiangmen, 26 Feb. 1928, MM.

19. J.E.W. to J.J. Considine, Baiqi, 30 Jan. 1927, MM.

20. Meagher to Curran, [New York?], 23 Jan. 1926; Meagher to Rt. Rev. William Quinn, Dir. SPF, [New York], 1 Aug. 1926, OPDC; V. Rev. Raymond Meagher, O.P., to Rev. L.F. Kearney, O.P., New York, 7 May 1924; James G. O'Donnell, O.P., to Meagher, Newark, N.J., 16 May 1927, OPDC; Edward Hughes, O.P., to Meagher, New York, 7 June 1927, OPDC; William A. Griffin, Diocesan Director [Newark], "Plan of Co-operation between the Diocese of Newark and the Missionary Training Houses and Particular Mission Collecting Agencies," 18 Sept. 1928, OPDC.

21. Rev. Ildephonse Rutherford, O.F.M., three-page memo, [1932 or thereafter]; Bertha L. Buehler to V. Rev. Vincent Schrempp, O.F.M., Zibo, Shandong, 27 Dec. 1927, OFMStL.

22. W.F. O'Shea, M.M., to J.E.W., [Maryknoll], 15 Oct. 1926 MM; J.A. Walsh to J.E.W., [Maryknoll], 26 Nov. 1926, MM.

23. J.E.W. to J.A. Walsh, Baiqi, 10 Jan. 1927, MM; J.E.W. to J.A. Walsh, Baiqi, 3 March 1927, MM.

24. J.E.W. to J.A. Walsh, Jiangmen, 1 June 1927: J.A. Walsh to J.E.W., [Maryknoll], 6 Sept. 1927, MM.

25. J.E.W. to J.A. Walsh, Baiqi, 3 March 1927; J.A. Walsh to J.E.W. [Maryknoll], 25 May 1927, MM. See also J.A. Walsh to J.E.W., [Maryknoll], 19 Oct. 1927, MM.

26. J.J. Corbett, C.M., to Joseph Illig (?), C.M., Ganzhou, 7 March 1927, CMJ.

27. The sisterhoods were the Sisters of Charity from Mount St. Joseph, Ohio; the Franciscan Sisters of Perpetual Adoration from La Crosse, Wisconsin; the Sisters of Notre Dame de Namur from Reading, Ohio; and the Sisters of Saint Francis from Luxemburg. From an obituary of Bishop Sylvester Espelage, *Franciscans in China* 13 (1940): 103–7. On the question of a surplus of Sisters in the Midwest, see Thomas A. Bowdern, S.J., "A Study of Vocations: An Investigation into the Environmental Factors of Vocations to the Priesthood and the Religious Life in the United States from 1919 to 1929" (Ph.D. dissertation, St. Louis University, 1936), pp. 44, 66 ff.; E. J. Boyd Barrett, "The Sociology of Nunneries," p. 175.

Chapter 5

1. [W.J. Downs, M.M.], "Enforced Silent Night," p. 42. I adopt here the date given in Shantou (R.L. Smyth) to Beijing (Macmurray), 22 Nov. 1929, 393.1163 Am3/85, USNA/RG 59. See also *Foreign Relations of the United States*, 1929, II, pt. 2, p. 489.

2. When the Sisters returned to Mei Xian in company with Fr. Downs, they passed through one town whose people asked who was the foreign devil with so many wives. See H.M. Bush to Fr. General, Souluo, 3 Dec. 1933, MM.

3. Ganzhou Vicariate Apostolic, "Spiritual Returns, 1 July—30 June, 1926, 1927 1928," CMJ; Wm J. McClimont, C.M., to Crusaders, St. Vincent's Seminary, Philadelphia, Dahoujiang, 5 Aug. 1928, CMJ; F.J. Stauble to Crusaders, Ganzhou, 1 July 1928, CMJ.

4. American Consul General, Guangzhou (Jenkins), to Secretary of State, 8 Feb. 1929, enclosure, 393.1111/Young, Edw./2, USNA/RG59.

5. Rev. Edw. M. Young, C.M., Diary, Nananfu, 22 Jan. 192[9?], CMJ; Secretary of State to the Minister in China (Macmurray), Washington, 24 Jan. 1929, 393.1111 Young, Edward/1; the Minister in China (Macmurray) to the Secretary of State, Beijing, 25 Jan. 1929, *Foreign Relations of the United States*, 1929, II, pp. 438-440; Wm. J. McClimont, C.M., to Vincentians at St. Vincent's Seminary, Philadelphia, Dahoujiang, 24 Feb. 1929, CMJ.

6. Ibid.; Jos. A. Gately, C.M., to confreres, [Jiangxi?], 23 May 1929, CMJ.

7. J.J. Corbett, C.M., to confreres in Philadelphia, Ganzhou, 17 March 1929; Minister in China to the Secretary of State, Beijing, 25 March 1929, 393.11/908, USNA/RG59; J.A. O'Shea to Consul General, Guangzhou, Ganzhou, 23 March 1929, 393.1163 Am3/66, USNA/RG59.

8. O'Shea to F.P. Lockhart, Ganzhou, 18 April 1929, 393.1163 Am3/73, USNA/RG59.

9. Wm. J. McClimont, C.M., to Rev. Thomas O'Connor, Ganzhou, 4 Aug. 1929, CMJ; J.A. Gately, C.M., to Crusaders, Xinfeng, 13 July 1929, CMJ; J.A. Gately, C.M., to confreres, Xinfeng, 24 July 1929, CMJ.

10. Con. Gen. at Wuhan to the Secretary of State, 6 Aug. 1929, 393.1163/342, in *Foreign Relations of the United States*, 1929, II, pp. 469-70.

11. Chargé in China (Perkins) to the Secretary of State, 25 Jan. 1930, 393.11/1057, in *Foreign Relations of the United States*, 1930, II, pp. 82-83.

12. J.A. O'Shea to Fr. Lynch, C.M., Ganzhou, 6 Dec. 1929, CMJ.

13. J.A. O'Shea to F.P. Lockhart, American consul, Wuhan, Ganzhou, 8 Feb. 1930, CMJ.

14. J.A. O'Shea, Diary, 15-21 March 1930, CMJ.

15. Of the Sisters' new foundation in Dawoli, about twenty-five miles from Ganzhou, J.A. O'Shea had written: "When the Sisters come and the pagans have more concrete examples of what the faith stands for, we expect conversions to be greatly increased." The Sisters were not responsible for the scale of the building. That was Fr. Dougherty's doing. The Sisters did dispensary work in Dawoli and Ganzhou. See J.A. O'Shea to confrere, Tangjiang, 29 Feb. 1929; Larry Curtis, C.M., to Ray Machate, Dawoli, 29 Jan. 1929; on the destruction of the mission stations, see F.J. Stauble, C.M., to confrere, Ganzhou, 25 Apr. 1930, CMJ.

16. F.J. Stauble, C.M., to confrere, Ganzhou, 25 Apr. 1930, CMJ.

17. J.A. O'Shea to Fr. Lynch, C.M., Ganzhou, 8 July 1931; Leon Cahill, C.M., to C.M. Crusaders, Philadelphia, Ganzhou, 6 Aug. 1930; Joe [Joseph A. Gately, C.M.] to "Nabz" [Fr. Lynch, C.M.], Jiangmen, Guangdong, 16 Oct. 1931, CMJ.

18. J.A. O'Shea to Fr. Lynch, C.M., Ganzhou, 3 Nov. 1931, CMJ.

19. J.A. Gately to confreres, 3 March 1932, CMJ; Beijing (Perkins) to the Secretary of State, 7 Feb. 1932, 393.11/1415 and Beijing (Perkins) to the Secretary of State, 8 Feb. 1932, 393.11/1420, cited in Julius Schick, pp. 67-68. O'Shea, however, later denied contacting the consul and claimed that the rapidity of the Nationalist government's response was based on its unwillingness to lend any justification to Japanese claims about disorder in China at the time of the Shanghai Incident. See O'Shea to Lynch, Ganzhou, 3 Apr. 1932, CMJ. O'Shea's memory was faulty. He had telegraphed the consul for help on February 5 or 6. See Schick, p. 67.

20. Larry Curtis, C.M., to Confreres, Tangjiang, 13 Apr. 1932, CMJ; Frank [Stauble] to Gerard, Ganzhou, 27 Jan. 1933, CMJ.

21. P. Misner to Fr. Winne, Yujiang, 22 Sept. 1938, CMStL; P. Curran to R. Meagher, Nandai, 12 Jan. 1929, OPDC; American consul general, Wuhan (F.P. Lockhart) to Secretary of State, No. 841, 9 Aug. 1928, 393.1163 Am3/48, and attached notes dated 24 Sept. and 26 Sept. 1928, USNA/RG59.

22. Legation to the Secretary of State, 2 Apr. 1931, 393.1163/489, USNA/RG59; Adams (Wuhan) to Johnson (Beijing), 23 May 1933, 393.1163 Am3/169, USNA/RG59, cited in Schick, p. 42. Citing Sheehan to Walter A. Adams, Yujiang, 30 May 1933, 393.1163 Am3/159, USNA/RG59, Schick notes (p. 41) that Sheehan "realized that the missionaries in his vicariate had suffered more at the hands of the Nationalist soldiers than at the hands of the Communists." Propaganda Fide reduced Sheehan's worries on November 29, 1932, when it detached five subprefectures of the Yujiang vicariate apostolic's territory around Nancheng (Qianchang). It called the new mission territory the prefecture apostolic of Qianchangfu and entrusted it to the Irish Columban Fathers. Sheehan himself died in September 1933, and in December 1934, Rome appointed Paul B. Misner, C.M., to succeed him.

23. Missionary Sisters of St. Mary's, "Intimate Sketches of Life in Foochow," *The Torch* 20:4 (Jan. 1936): 19; Anon., ms. history of Jian'ou mission, n.d., pp. 6, 3, OPDC; American consul, Fuzhou (Burke), to Secretary of State, 24 Dec. 1931, 393.1163/540, USNA/RG59; Anon., ms. history of the Jian'ou mission, n.d., p. 7, OPDC.

24. D. Langenbacher to Fr. Provincial, Yuanling, 25 Nov. 1927, CPUC; Anthony Maloney, C.P., "In Line of Duty: An Account of the Tragedy," in *Eyes East*, pp. 9-11.

25. Stanislaus Grennan, C.P., to William F. Montavon, Director, Legal Department, National Catholic Welfare Conference, Union City, N.J., 4 May 1929, CPUC.

26. Jeremiah McNamara, C.P., "Cholera Claims Sister Devota," in *Eyes East*, pp. 38-42.

27. Freundt, pp. 62-65.
28. Ibid., p. 78.
29. Ibid., pp. 62, 68, 70; Sr. M. Dominica to Rev. Mother, Wuchang, 30 June 1933, FSPA; Sr. M. Stella to Rev. Mother, Wuchang, 7 July 1935; Sr. M. Dominica to Rev. Mother, Wuchang, 10 July 1935; Sr. M. Ceciline to Rev. Mother, Wuchang, [1931], FSPA.
30. Between 1933 and 1951 the Sisters' Shanghai school would serve students of thirty-three nationalities of which the three largest groups were Chinese, English, and Portugese. By the time the Sisters were interned by the Japanese on April 1, 1943, in Shanghai Refugee Camp 3, the school had been in four different locations. Gutteres, pp. 86-126 and passim.
31. McDonald, pp. 20-21, 31, 34-35.
32. "Mother M. Gratia—Valiant Woman," in *Fifty Years* [Taizhong, 1970?], pp. 11-12.
33. Ibid., p. 14.
34. Ambrose Pinger, O.F.M., to Fr. Provincial, Zhoucun, 21 Sept. 1932, OFMStL.
35. *Fu Jen Magazine* 4 (Jan. 1935): frontispiece.
36. Sr. Ronayne Gergen, O.S.B., interview with the author, Taibei, Taiwan, 2 Nov. 1971.
37. Fr. Arnold Janssen, a German secular priest of the Muenster diocese, founded the Society of the Divine Word at Steyl, Holland, in 1875. His purpose was to draw together the German secular priests exiled by Bismarck's *Kulturkampf* and to raise the desperately low spirits of the German Catholic community. It was Janssen's primary aim to save the Catholic Church in Germany by using a mission to China as a means of rekindling and refocusing German Catholicism's energies and providing it with a sense of shared purpose. By 1923 Divine Word society members, also known as Steyl Fathers, were operating missions in Shandong, Gansu, and Henan provinces. American members were operating a mission in Xinxiang, Henan. See Hogan, Fecher, pp. 923-24; Edward J. Wojniak, *Atomic Apostle* (Techny, Ill.: Divine Word Publications, 1957).
38. Shearman and Sterling, a law firm at 55 Wall St., New York City, to Department of State, 10 Aug. 1937, 393.1164 "Benedictine Society," USNA/RG59. National City Bank of New York was the chief aggrieved creditor.
39. "Excerpts from the Chronicle of the Catholic University of Peking," *Fu Jen Magazine* 4 (Oct. 1935): 160.
40. The first Maryknoller arrived in 1925 and five more in both 1927 and 1929. See J.M. Blois, vicar apostolic of Shenyang, to S. Cong. de Prop. Fide, "Renseignements Sur La Future Mission de 'Tung Pien Tao,' " Machecoul (France), 18 June 1930, MM. On the financial question see R.A. Lane to John [Considine?], Fushun, 7 Jan. 1928; J.P. McCormack to J.A. Walsh, Fushun, 11 Apr. 1930, MM.
41. R.A. Lane to John [Considine?], Fushun, 7 Jan. 1928, MM.
42. J.M. Blois to S. Cong. de Prop. Fide, "Renseignements Sur La Future Mission de 'Tung Pien Tao,' " Machecoul, 18 June 1930; J.P. McCormack to Most Rev. Celso Costantini, Fushun, 29 July 1930; see also addendum to same letter, 6 Aug 1930, MM.
43. J.P. McCormack to Celso Costantini, Fushun, 29 July 1930, MM.
44. J.P. McCormack to J.A. Walsh, Fushun, 6 Aug. 1930, MM.
45. J.A. Walsh to J.P. McCormack, Maryknoll, 25 Sept. 1931, MM; R.A. Lane to J.A. Walsh, Fushun, 7 Apr. 1933; "Fushun Junior Seminary, Scholastic Year—September 1932 to July 1933, Rev. John F. Walsh, M.M. (?) [sic]," MM; John F. Walsh to Wm. F. O'Shea, Linjiang, 1 Nov. 1933, MM.

46. Fr. Sylvio R. Gilbert, M.M., to Maryknoll, Dandong, 11 Jan. 1928, MM; Leo Davis to J.A. Walsh, Dandong, 11 Jan. 1928, MM.

47. Gerard A. Donovan to J.A. Walsh, Xinbin, 22 Nov. 1931, MM; John Comber to J.A. Walsh, Tonghua, 20 May 1932, MM.

48. Walter Coleman, M.M., to J.P. McCormack, Linjiang, 16 July 1932, MM.

49. Fr. Bridge, "Manchuria 1931-1932," Xinbin, received at Maryknoll, 8 Aug. 1932; Rev. Alonso Escalante, Xinbin Manchuria Diary, Oct. 1932; Thomas M. Quirk to J.A. Walsh, Erbashi, 5 Aug. 1932; R.A. Lane to J.A. Walsh, Fushun, 23 Feb. 1933, MM.

50. The Fushun mission operation was indeed extensive. The mission territory embraced 32,000 square miles with a population of about 5,000,000. To look after the 4402 Catholics and 3086 catechumens there were during 1932 and 1933 twenty Maryknoll and five Chinese priests, two Maryknoll Brothers, and nineteen Sisters, twelve of them Maryknollers. The mission personnel also included nineteen virgins, twenty-seven aspirants to the sisterhood, forty-five catechists, and thirty baptizers. These were spread out over eighty-eight mission stations, a prep seminary, five orphanages, seven dispensaries, twenty-four elementary, nine prayer, and two industrial schools. "Report of the Prefecture Apostolic of Fushun, Manchuria, 1932-1933," MM.

51. *Shengching Shibao*, "Catholic Priests in a Position of Service Suspicion," Shenyang, 21 Nov. 1933, copy in MM.

52. "Summary of action taken in reference to the article which appeared in the Sheng Ching Shih Pao and other papers; November 21, 1933"; R. A. Lane to J. A. Walsh, Fushun, 10 April 1934, MM.

53. J.J. Corbet to Novice Richard A. Loeffler, n.C.M., Ganzhou, 19 April 1928, CMJ.

54. Fr. Buckley, M.M. to Maryknoll, Pingnan, Guangxi, 20 Feb. 1929, MM.

55. J.E.W. "Report of the Kongmoon [Jiangmen] Vicariate for General Chapter, August, 1929," MM; J.E.W. to J.A. Walsh, Jiangmen, 4 April 1929, MM.

56. J.E.W. "Report of the Kongmoon [Jiangmen] Vicariate for General Chapter, August, 1929," MM.

57. Joseph McGinn, Chiqi Mission Diary, Nov. 1930, Feb. 1931, April 1931, MM.

58. J.E.W. to J.A. Walsh, Jiangmen, 25 May 1931, MM; J.E.W., "[Jiangmen] Spiritual Returns, 1931," MM; J.E.W., "Maryknoll in Kongmoon, 1932." MM.

Chapter 6

1. William J. Downs, "Enforced Silent Night" (ms, MM), p. 132.

2. Sr. Mary Sheridan, M.M., interview with the author, Gongguang, Taiwan, 1 Dec. 1971.

3. Lazaristes du Peit'ang, p. 419.

4. [J.J. Considine] to J.E.W., Rome, 2 Sept. 1933, MM.

5. C.D. Simons, S.J., to Z.J. Maher, Suzhou (Suchow), Jiangsu, 2 Sept. 1933, SJLG. This view is diametrically opposed to that of the first American Jesuit in China, Hornsby, who held to the belief current in Hong Kong in 1893 that only if merchants opened the way by inducing a taste for occidental things could missioners gain entry into interior China. See WL 22:1 (1893): 21-22. In the twentieth century, the Hornsby viewpoint was not the majority viewpoint among American Catholic missionaries.

6. George Dunne, S.J., to Z.J. Maher, S.J., Xujiawei, 19 Nov. 1932, SJLG. The French Jesuit superior kept Mr. Dunne at Xujiawei to study Chinese.

7. George Dunne, S.J., "A Brief Summary of the Need for, and the Objective of, the Nanking Project, and the Means to the End Proposed," SJLG.

8. Ibid.; J.F. Kearney, S.J., to Fr. Provincial, Shanghai, 3 Dec. 1934, Ralph Deward, S.J., to Z.J. Maher, S.J., Xujiawei, 11 Feb. 1935, SJLG.

9. J.F. Kearney, S.J., to Mrs. Everman, Nanjing, 22 June 1941, Simons Papers, SJLG.

10. Thomas V. Kiernan, "Opportunities," Pingnan, 20 April 1934, MM.

11. Frank Stauble, C.M., to Jim Culbert, Ganzhou, 16 Aug. 1933; Frederick A. McGuire to Ed [Kiernan], Ganzhou, 13 Sept. 1933; Munday to confreres, Tangjiang, 19 Feb. 1934, CMJ.

12. Fr. Moehringer, C.M., to Fr. Lynch, C.M., n.p., 14 June 1934, CMJ.

13. John Munday, C.M., to Fr. O'Connor, C.M., Tangjiang, 6 Feb. 1935, CMJ.

14. Larry Curtis, C.M., to Eugene, Dawoli, 30 Jan. 1936, CMJ.

15. Larry Curtis, C.M., to James Collins, C.M., Ganzhou, 18 June 1937, CMJ.

16. American consul, Fuzhou (Burke), to the Secretary of State, 1 Nov. 1933, 393.1163 Am3/189, USNA/RG59.

17. American consul, Fuzhou (Burke) to American legation, Beijing, 5 Feb. 1934 393.63/670; Johnson to Wang Zhaoming, Beijing, 3 March 1934, 393.1163/672; Fuzhou (Burke) to American legation, Beijing, 4 April 1934, 393.1163/679, USNA/RG59; American consul, Fuzhou (Burke), to the Secretary of State, 3 May 1934, 393.1163 Am/196, USNA/RG59.

18. Missionary Sister, "Intimate Sketches of Life in Foochow," *The Torch* 20:4 (Jan. 1936): 19; Lazaristes de Peit'ang, pp. 377-78.

19. St. Mary's of the Springs Mission in China," *The Torch* 19:7 (April 1935): 16-17; anon. ms. history of the Jian'ou mission, n.d., n.p., p. 12, OPDC; *The Torch* 21:11 (Sept. 1937): 28.

20. "Bonny" [Bonaventure Griffiths], C.P., to "Andy" [Rev.Andrew Ansbro, C.P.], Yuanling, 14 June 1935, CPUC. Not all the contact between Communist forces and missionaries in this area was hostile. According to Gregory McEttrick, stationed in Yongsui, the missionaries often cared for sick and wounded Communist soldiers, thereby earning the respect and appreciation of the Communists. Gregroy McEttrick, C.P., to author, summer survey, 1970.

21. Lazaristes du Peit'ang, pp. 329-31.

22. Ibid., pp. 313-315.

23. McDonald, pp. 38-40.

24. Lazaristes du Peit'ang, pp. 105-6; anon., "Only a Mission Nurse," n.p., [1934?], ASC; Sr. Sophie, "A Year in China," [1934?], ASC; Catholic Directory 1937, p. 647.

25. "Propagation of the Faith Ordinary Subsidy Comparative Reports," MM.

26. "Fushun Mission Report, 1933-34"; [J.J. Considine?] to R.A. Lane, Rome, 13 Feb., 1934, MM.

27. Lazaristes du Peit'ang, pp. 31-33; Fr. Escalante to J.A. Walsh, Tonghua, 30 July 1934, MM.

28. R.A. Lane to J.A. Walsh, Dalian, 17 Oct. 1934; R.A. Lane to Fr. Drought, Dalian, 5 Nov. 1934, MM.

29. J.A. Walsh to R.A. Lane, [Maryknoll], 23 Nov. 1934, MM.

30. J.M. Drought to R.A. Lane, [Maryknoll], 11 Oct 1935; R.A. Lane to J.E. Walsh, Fushun, 2 March 1937. MM.

31. *Fu Jen Magazine* 4 (Jan. 1935): frontispiece; 7 (Aug. 1938): 116-17.

32. Ibid., 4 (Oct. 1935): 159; 8 (Jan. 1939): 16.

33. [J.J. Considine] to J.E.W., Rome, 2 Sept. 1933, MM.

Chapter 7

1. Joseph P. McGinn to J.E.W., Dongzhen, 1 Nov. 1937, MM; A.J. Paschang to J.E.W., Jiangmen, 11 Dec. 1937, MM; John Lima, M.M., to Tom [Kiernan?], Luoding, 25 Feb. 1939, MM; R.P. Kennelly to Fr. Drought, Luoding, 12 March 1939, MM.

2. American Consul, Fuzhou (Ward) to the Secretary of State, 11 July 1941, 393.1163 Am3/368; F.A. McGuire, C.M., to Bob, C.M., Yudu, 19 July 1939, CMJ.

3. American Consul, Kumming (Yunnanfu) (Brown), to Secretary of State, 28 Aug. 1940, 393.1163 Am3/547, USNA.RG59; O'Gara to Vice-Consul, Kunming (Yunnanfu), Yuanling, 13 Aug. 1940, CPUC; Tokyo (Grew) to Secretary of State, 30 Sept. 1940, 393.1163 Am3/547, USNA/RG59; American Consul General, Shanghai (Butrick) to Secretary of State, No. 3428, 12 Sept. 1940, 393.1163 Am 3/545; Tokyo (Grew) to Secretary of State, 30 Sept. 1940, 393.1163 Am3/548; Tokyo (Grew) to Secretary of State, 17 June 1941, 393.1163 Am3/620, USNA/RG59; American Consul General, Shanghai, to Secretary of State, 29 Sept. 1941, 393.1163 Am3/647, USNA/RG59. For a list of more than 240 bombing incidents involving American-owned property and Japanese planes, see 393.1163/1186, USNA/RG59. The twenty-three page list, however, is not complete.

4. American Consul, Fuzhou (Rice) to Secretary of State, telegram, 14 Oct. 1941, 393.1163 Am3/632, USNA/RG59; a Vincentian to confreres, Longnan, 25 Nov. 1941, CMJ.

5. J.E.W. to Council Members, Hong Kong, 10 Nov. 1938, MM.

6. John R. O'Donnell to J.E.W., *M.S. Gripsholm*, 22 Aug. 1942, MM.

7. J.C. Burns to T.V. Kiernan, Fushun, 23 Sept. 1938, MM; A.J. Paschang to J.E.W., Hong Kong, 11 June 1940, MM.

8. McDonald, pp. 53-58.

9. Sr. Mary Louise Utar, A.S.C., "Concentration Period of our Nine Sisters in China, December 8, 1941—August 17, 1945," ASC; Fr. Boniface Pfeilschifter, O.F.M., "Fr. Boniface's Story," in Fr. Norbert Schmalz, O.F.M., and Boniface Pfeilschifter, O.F.M., *Shen Fu's Story* (Chicago: Franciscan Herald Press, 1966), pp. 135-67, provides a narration of events after the Japanese entry into the Zibo vicariate apostolic.

10. McDonald, pp. 53-58.

11. *Fifty Years*, p. 21; Sr. M. Gratia to Rev. Mother M. Raphael, Kaifeng, 24 Jan. 1938; Sr. M. Gratia to Rev. Mother M. Bernard, Kaifeng, 26 June 1940, SPSM; McDonald, pp. 48-50.

12. B.C. Werner to T.S. McDermott, Jian'ou 14 Feb. 1943, OPDC; Rev. Emmanuel Trainor, C.P., Mission Procurator, to Msgr. Thomas J. McDonnell, National Director of the Society of the Propagation of the Faith, Union City, N.J., 9 July 1942, CPUC.

13. Wojniak, *Atomic Apostle*, pp. 85-89, 97-98; A.J. Paschang to Fr. General, Wuzhou, 19 Oct. 1942, MM.

14. A. Pinger, O.F.M., to Fr. Provincial, Zhoucun, 6 June 1939, OFMStL; C. O'Gara, C.P., "Quinquennial Report, Diocese of Yuanling," p. 2, CPUC.

15. J.E.W. to A.J. Paschang, (Maryknoll), 6 Apr. 1940, MM.

16. Bauer, p. 77; J.E.W. to Council Members, n. p., 19 June 1939, MM.

17. Misner to Steve Dunker, C.M., Yujiang, 26 Feb. 1936, CMStL; Misner to Fr. Winne, Yujiang, 10 Aug. 1938, CMStL.

18. F.J. Stauble, C.M., to Mr. John A. Ryan, C.M., Ganzhou, 8 Oct. 1938, CMJ.

19. F.J. Stauble, C.M., to Confrere, Ganzhou, 5 Aug. 1941, CMJ; J.A. Gately, C.M., to Fr. Murray, C.M., Nangan, 11 Oct. 1941, CMJ.

20. L. Curtis, C.M., to Vincentian Novices, Tangjiang, 22 July 1942, CMJ; Joseph Kennedy, C.M., to Walter, C.M., Dahujiang, 6 July 1941, CMJ.

21. [W. J. Downs], "Enforced Silent Night," pp. 127, 138, 152, MM.

22. *Fu Jen Magazine* 7 (May 1938): 75, 8 (June 1939): p. 89, 8 (Dec. 1939): 152; Rev. Richard Arens, S.V.D., interview with the author, Fu Ren University, Xinzhuang, Taiwan, 28 Nov. 1971.

23. B.C. Werner to T.S. McDermott, Jian'ou, 14 Feb. 1943, OPDC.

24. A.J. Paschang to J.M. Drought, Gaozhou, 30 Apr. 1943, MM.

25. [J.E.W.] to Considine, Kunming, 23 Sept. 1944; J.J. C[onsidine] to Bp. Paschang, 16 Oct. 1944; Kunming Mission Diary, 1, 7, 11, 20 Nov. 1944, MM; Foreign Claims Settlement Commission of the United States, Claim No. W-10657 cited in Decision No. CN-448, and Claim No. W-7010 cited in Decision No. CN-466.

26. [J.E.W.] to Wm. P. Langdon, Am. consul, Kunming, Kunming, 17 Jan. 1945, MM; Michael Ready, Gen. Scty., National Catholic Welfare Conference, to Maxwell Anderson, Chief, Division of Far Eastern Affairs, Department of State, Washington, D.C., 30 Oct. 1941, USNA/RG65, 393.1163 AM 3/640.

27. [J.E.W.] to Considine, Kunming, Yunnan, China, 14 Dec. 1944, MM.

28. Kerrison, pp. 229, 230.

29. J.E.W. to A. J. Paschang, Maryknoll, 26 May 1943, MM; Cuthbert O'Gara, Address to the Twenty-Eighth Provincial Chapter, 12 July 1944, CPUC; Wojniak, *Atomic Apostle*, pp. 148-55.

30. Ibid., p. 145; Rev. Joseph Stier, S.V.D., interview with the author, Fu Jen University, Xinzhuang, Taiwan, 29 Nov. 1971; William E. Barrett, pp. 359-60, 362; Rev. Edwin McCabe, M.M., interview with the author, Miaoli, Taiwan, 1 Dec. 1971; Regis Boyle, C.P., to Rev. Emmanuel Trainor, C.P., Beijing, 18 Dec. 1946, CPUC.

31. Bp. Cuthbert O'Gara, C.P., D.D., Bishop of Yuanling, Hunan. Address delivered before the Cardinal Mindszenty Foundation Third Annual Conference, St. Louis, Mo., 28 March 1965, CPUC.

32. George Haggerty, M.M., to Fr. General, Tianjin, 16 Aug. 1947, MM.

33. Fr. Dietz to Archbishop Nigris, n.p., 31 Jan. 1947, MM. J.P. McCormack to Fr. Walsh, Fushun, 27 Feb. 1947, MM. Unsworth, p. 66. Boniface Pfeilschifter in Schmalz and Pfeilschifter, pp. 173, 171. Sr. Mary Louise Utar, A.S.C., to author; Sr. Mary Regis Zarr, A.S.C., to author; Sr. Mary Colette Woltering, A.S.C., to author; Sr. Maureen Shay, A.S.C., to author; Sr. Mary Edward Pessina, A.S.C., to author; Sr. Mary Anthony Mathews, A.S.C., to author; Sr. Mary Ellen Brundza, A.S.C., to author, summer survey, 1970. Pfeilschifter in Schmalz and Pfeilschifter, pp. 177-86.

34. Wojniak, pp. 153-55, 162, 168, 173, 176 ff., 202-3.

35. Unsworth, p. 49; Paul Curran to T.S. McDermott, Jian'ou, 12 July 1948, OPDC; Jian'ou, 29 Apr. 1949, OPDC; Hong Kong, 13 June 1949, OPDC.

36. Francis O'Neill, M.M., unpublished memoirs; Paul J. Duchesne, M.M., interview with the author, Taibei, 23 Nov. 1971.

37. T. Labrador to T.S. McDermott, Fuzhou, 30 June 1949, OPDC. Stephen B. Edmonds, M.M., the author's 1970 summer survey. Linus Lombard, C.P., interview with the author, Union City, N.J., 21 Nov. 1970.

38. Herbert Elliott, M.M., the author's 1970 summer survey. Robert Kennelly,

M.M., the author's 1970 summer survey. Donald E. MacInnes, ed., *Religious Policy and Practice in Communist China: A Documentary History* (New York: Macmillan, 1972), p. 21.

39. Cuthbert O'Gara, C.P., "Address before the Twentieth National Convention: Catholic War Veterans of America," New York, 20 Aug. 1955, CPUC. Leon Sullivan, O.F.M., interview with the author, Washington D.C., 23 Aug. 1970. Linus Lombard, C.P., nodded his assent when asked: "With the exception of the threat of violence, was, as Fr. Leon Sullivan believes, brainwashing like the novitiate?" in an interview with the author, Union City, N.J., 21 Nov. 1970. Fr. John Clifford, S.J., while admitting to the basic similarities between the novitiate experience and the "brainwashing" experience, stressed that the threat of violence hanging over the participants in the Chinese Communists propaganda sessions differentiated the two experiences, in an interview with the author, Los Gatos, Cal., 3 Sept. 1971.

Chapter 8

1. J.E.W., "Report of the Kongmoon Vicariate for General Chapter, August, 1929," MM.

2. Sr. Dominica, F.S.P.A., to Rev. Mother, on board the *Poyang* (British steamer) on the Chang Jiang, 23 Oct. 1928, FSPA.

3. Frank Melvin, C.M., to Fr. John [Lynch?], Tangjiang, 18 Feb. 1934, CMJ. Joseph Kennedy, C.M., to Walter, C.M., Dahujiang, 6 July 1941, CMJ. George Dunne, S.J., "A Brief Summary of the Need for, and Objective of, the Nanking Project, and the Means to the End Proposed," SJLG.

4. Crane, passim.

5. J.A. Gately, C.M., to Crusaders, Xinfeng, 13 July 1929, CMJ.

6. [J.A. Walsh], "The Pioneer's Log," *The Field Afar* 12:6 (June 1918): 86.

7. Sr. Vincent Louis De Lude, *Diary*, p. 1. Archives, Daughters of Charity, Emmitsburg, Md.

8. Bowdern, p. 402.

9. Ibid., p. 177.

10. *Catholic Missions* 2 (March 1935): 69-70.

11. Among the sixty-eight priests who responded to the author's summer 1970 survey, the average age of entrance into the seminary was 17.7; median age was 18.8. Only nine of the respondents entered after their twenty-first birthday and none of the thirty-two who entered the seminary with the desire to go to China entered after 1928. The average age at which those who entered the seminary first entertained that desire to go to China was 14.1. The median year of their entrance into the seminary was 1921. The median year of entrance was 1927 for those who entered the seminary with no desire to go to China. The average age of entrance into the convent of the thirty-five women missionaries reporting was 19.7. Median age of the responding missionary Sisters upon entrance into the convent was 19.

12. The militant hymn of the Catholic Students Mission Crusade, which Rev. Daniel A. Lord, S.J., wrote, mingled religion and patriotism: "Comrades true/Dare and do/'Neath the Queen's White and Blue/For our Flag/For our Faith/For Christ the King. . . ." Cited in Caryl Rivers, *Aphrodite at Mid-Century: Growing up Catholic and Female in Post-War America* (Garden City, N.Y.: Doubleday, 1973), pp. 117-18.

13. Eberhardt, p. 444.

14. John LaFarge, S.J., to Zacheus J. Maher, S.J., New York, 30 Aug. 1939, John LaFarge, S.J., Papers, Lavinger Collection, Georgetown University.

15. George M. Willman, S.J., "Stopping the Leakage," *WL* 55 (1926): 366-77;

Brother Henry Barthelemy, O.P., "Rural Catholics," *Dominicana* 9 (Dec. 1924): 38-48. The Jesuit Father C.C. Martindale believed that the Church's ban on contraception was driving thousands of Catholics from the Church. See E. J. Boyd Barrett, *While Peter Sleeps*, p. 23; Eliot, pp. 267-81.

16. NCWC release, 9 May 1938, in USNA/RG59 393.1111/.56 (M) Donovan, Gerard.

17. Bowdern, "A Study of Vocations," pp. 44, 68ff; E.J. Boyd Barrett, "The Sociology of Nunneries," p. 175.

18. R. Meagher, O.P., to Paul Curran, O.P., New York, 27 Jan. 1926, OPDC.

19. J. Corbett, C.M., to President, CSMC-Germantown, Ganzhou, 16 May 1926, CMJ.

20. John J. Considine, M.M., commenting on a draft essay by John LaFarge, S.J., dated June 1944. See "Catholic Association for International Peace," folder No. 3-15, John LaFarge, S.J., Papers.

21. Ryan, p. 178.

22. Ibid., pp. 177-78

23. *Miami Herald*, 21 March 1979, p. A 1.

Principal Sources Consulted

Archives and Manuscript Collections

Adorers of the Blood of Christ, Ruma, Ill.
Daughters of Charity, Emmitsburg, Md.
Dominican Fathers, Washington, D.C.
Franciscan Fathers, St. Louis, Mo.
Franciscan Sisters of Perpetual Adoration, La Crosse, Wisc.
Jesuit Missions, Inc., New York, N.Y.
John LaFarge, S.J., Papers, Georgetown University, Washington, D.C.
Maryknoll Fathers, Maryknoll, N.Y.
Maryknoll Sisters' Mission Research Library, Rogers College, Maryknoll, N.Y.
Passionist Fathers, Union City, N.J.
Sisters of Providence, St. Mary of the Woods, Ind.
Sisters of St. Joseph, Baden, Pa.
Society of Jesus, California Province, Los Gatos, Cal.
United States, Department of State, Decimal File, National Archives, Washington, D.C.
Vincentian Fathers, Eastern Province, St. John's University, Jamaica, N.Y.
Vincentian Fathers, Western Province, St. Louis, Mo.

Select Bibliography

Atlas Hierarchicus, Supplement. Mödling, Austria: St. Gabriel Verlag, 1968.
Attwater, Rachel. *Adam Schall: A Jesuit at the Court of China, 1592–1666.* Adapted from the French of Joseph Duhr, S.J. London: Geoffrey Chapman, 1963.
Baker, Terrill. *Darkness of the Sun: The Story of Christianity in the Japanese Empire.* New York and Nashville: Abingdon-Cokesbury, 1947.
Barrett, E. J. Boyd, "The Sociology of Nunneries." *American Mercury* 34:2 (Feb. 1935).
———. *While Peter Sleeps.* New York: Washburn, 1929.
Barrett, William E. *The Red Lacquered Gate: The Story of Bishop Galvin, Co-Founder of the Columban Fathers.* New York: Sheed and Ward, 1967.
Bass, Harold James. "The Policy of the American State Department Toward Missionaries in the Far East." Ph.D. dissertation, State College of Washington, 1937.
Bauer, George, M.M. "The Often Circuitous Way of Divine Providence." Unpublished autobiography, 1969, MM.
Beaver, R. Pierce. *All Loves Excelling: American Protestant Women in World Mission.* Grand Rapids, Mich.: Eerdmans, 1968.
Borg, Dorothy. *American Policy and the Chinese Revolution, 1925–1928.* New York: American Institute of Pacific Relations and Macmillan, 1947.
Bowdern, Thomas S., S.J. "A Study of Vocations: An Investigation into the Environmental Factors of Vocations to the Priesthood and the Religious Life in

the United States from 1919 to 1929." Ph.D. dissertation, St. Louis University, 1936.

Breslin, Thomas A. "The Disordered Society: American Catholics Look at China, 1900–1937." M.A. thesis, University of Virginia, 1969.

Cary-Elwes, Columba. *China and the Cross: A Survey of Mission History.* New York: P. J. Kenedy & Sons, 1957.

Cassidy, William F., O.P. "Kienning Fu Chronicle." New York: Holy Rosary Foreign Mission Society, 1948.

Catholic Foreign Mission Society of America. *Maryknoll Mission Letters, China: Extracts from the letters and diaries of the pioneer missioners of the Catholic Foreign Mission Society of America.* New York: Macmillan, 1923–42 (Vol. 1, 1923; Vol. 2, 1927).

Chang, C., S.J. "Essai d'une adaptation des Exercices Spirituels a l'ame Chinois" (Excerpta ex dissertatione ad lauream in Facultate Theologicae, Pontificiae Universitatis Gregorianae). Rome, 1952.

Chang, Chi-yun, ed. *National Atlas of China.* Yang Min Shan, Taiwan: National War College, 1962.

Chih, Andre. *L'Occident "Chretien" vu par les Chinois vers La Fin Du XIXc Siecle (1870–1900).* Paris: Presses Universitaires de France, 1962.

Clark, Francis X. *The Purpose of Missions: A Study of the Mission Documents of the Holy See, 1909–1946.* New York: Missionary Union of the Clergy, 1948.

Coffey, Reginald, O.P. *The American Dominicans: A History of St. Joseph's Province.* New York: St. Martin de Porres Guild Press, 1970.

Cohen, Paul A. *China and Christianity: The Missionary Movement and the Growth of Chinese Antiforeignism, 1860–1870.* Cambridge, Mass.: Harvard University Press, 1963.

Colombel, Auguste, M., S.J. *Histoire de la Mission du Kiangnan,* vol. 3, *Du Pere Gotteland, 1840, a l'Episcopat de Mgr. Languillat.* Shanghai: Mission Catholique, 1895-1905, 6 vols.

Cousins, John W., C.P. "The Sign Magazine: A Study in Business Policy." Unpublished required second year research report, Harvard Business School, n.d.

Crane, Daniel M. "The United States and the Chinese Republic: Power, Profit, and the Politics of Benevolence." Ph.D. dissertation, University of Virginia, 1974.

Crapez, Henri, C.M. "Les Lazaristes et le Clerge Chinois de 1697 a 1900 (Notes D'Histoire)." *Revue D'Histoire Des Missions* 15:1 (March 1938).

Donovan, John F., M.M. *The Pagoda and the Cross: The Life of Bishop Ford of Maryknoll.* New York: Scribners, 1967.

Dorland, Albert A. "A Preliminary Study of the Role of the French Protectorate of Roman Catholic Missions in Sino-French Diplomatic Relations." M.A. thesis, Cornell University, 1951.

Dunne, George, S.J. *Generation of Giants: The Story of the Jesuits in China in the Last Decades of the Ming Dynasty.* Notre Dame, Ind.: University of Notre Dame Press, 1962.

Eberhardt, Auleen. "Catholic Students Mission Crusade." *Commonweal* 22 (6 Sept. 1935).

D'Elia, Pascal M., S.J. *Catholic Native Episcopacy in China: Being an Outline of the Formation and Growth of the Chinese Catholic Clergy, 1300–1926.* Zikawei, Shanghai: T'usewei Printing Press, 1927.

———, ed. *Fonti Ricciani: Documenti Originale Concernenti Matteo Ricci E La Storia Delle Prime Relazioni Tra L'Europa E La Cina (1579–1615).* Editi E Commentati Da Pasquale M. D'Elia, S.J. Vol. II. Rome, 1949.

Eliot, Lester P. "The Troubles of American Catholicism." *American Mercury* 34:135 (March 1935).

Ellis, John Tracy. *American Catholics and the Intellectual Life.* Chicago: Heritage Foundation, 1956.

──────, ed. *The Catholic Priest in the United States: Historical Investigations.* Collegeville, Minn.: St. John's University Press, 1971.

Erikson, Kai T. *Wayward Puritans: A Study in the Sociology of Deviance.* New York: Wiley, 1966.

Fecher, V.J. "Society of the Divine Word," *New Catholic Encyclopedia*, vol. 4. New York: McGraw-Hill, 1967.

Fei, Hsiao-tung. *Peasant Life in China.* London: Kegan Paul, 1967.

Fifty Years. [Taichung, Taiwan, 1970?]

Ford, Francis X., M.M. *Stone in the King's Highway: Selections from the Writings of Bishop Francis Xavier Ford (1892–1952).* With Introductory Memoir by Most Rev. Raymond A. Lane, M.M., D.D., Superior General of Maryknoll. New York: McMullen Books, 1953.

Freundt, Urban, O.F.M. "Our China Missions." *Provincial Chronicle of St. John the Baptist Province, Cincinnati* 4:2 (1931).

Galush, William. "The Polish National Catholic Church: A Survey of Its Origins, Development and Missions." *Records of the American Catholic Historical Society of Philadelphia* 83:3–4 (Sept.–Dec. 1972).

Gleason, Philip. *The Conservative Reformers: German-American Catholics and the Social Order.* Notre Dame, Ind.: University of Notre Dame Press, 1968.

Gonzales, Jose M., O.P. *Historia De Las Misiones Dominicanas De China, 1900–1954.* Madrid: Ediciones Studium, 1955.

Goodrich, L. Carrington. "American Catholic Missions in China," *Chinese Political and Social Science Review* 12 (1928).

Gregg, Alice H. *China and Educational Autonomy.* Syracuse, N.Y.: Syracuse University Press, 1946.

Gutteres, Sr. Antonella Marie, S.L. *Lorettine Education in China, 1923–1952: Educational Activities of the Sisters of Loretto in China, Hanyang and Shanghai.* Taipei: United Publishing Center, 1961.

Habig, Marion A., O.F.M. *Heralds of the King.* Chicago: Franciscan Herald Press, 1957.

──────. *In Journeyings Often: Franciscan Pioneers in the Orient.* St. Bonaventure, N.Y.: Franciscan Institute, 1953.

──────. *Pioneering in China: The Story of the Rev. Francis Xavier Engbring, O.F.M., The First Native American Priest in China, 1857–1895.* Chicago: Franciscan Herald Press, 1930.

Hales, E.E.Y. *The Catholic Church and the Modern World.* Garden City, N.Y.: Hanover House, 1958.

Hay, Malcolm. *Failure in the Far East: Why and How the Breach Between the Western World and China First Began.* London: Neville Spearman, ca. 1956.

Hazelrigg, Lawrence E. "Occupation and Religious Practice in Italy: The Thesis of 'Working-Class Alienation.' " *Journal for the Scientific Study of Religion* 11:4 (Dec. 1972).

Hermand, Louis, S.J. *Les Etapes de la Mission Du Kiang-Nan, 1842–1922, Chine; Jesuites; Province de France.* Zikawei: T'ou-se-wei, 1926.

Hickey, Edward John. *The Society for the Propagation of the Faith: Its Foundation, Organization, and Success (1822–1922).* The Catholic University of America Studies in American Church History, vol. 3. Washington, D.C.: Catholic University of America, 1922.

Hinton, William. *Fanshen: A Documentary of Revolution in a Chinese Village.* New York: Vintage Books, 1966.

Hogan, Bro. Patrick, S.V.D. "The Society of the Divine Word in China: A Case Study." Unpublished essay, Seton Hall University, 1970.

Hoyt, Frederick B. "Americans in China and the Formation of American Policy, 1925–1937." Ph.D. dissertation, University of Wisconsin, 1971.

Hsu, Francis L.K. *Americans and Chinese*. Garden City, N.Y.: Doubleday, 1970.

Hsü, Immanuel C.Y. *The Rise of Modern China*, 2d ed. New York: Oxford, 1975.

Jeanne Marie, Sister. *Maryknoll's First Lady*. Garden City, N.Y.: Doubleday, 1967.

Jen, Yu-wen, *The Taiping Revolutionary Movement*. New Haven: Yale University Press, 1973.

Keller, James and Berger, Meyer. *Men of Maryknoll*. New York: Grosset and Dunlap, 1944.

Kerrison, Raymond. *Bishop Walsh of Maryknoll*. New York: Lancer Books, 1963.

King, Clifford J., S.V.D. "The Protestant Breakdown in China." *America* 38 (5 Nov. 1927).

Kirsch, Felix M., O.F.M., Cap. *The Spiritual Direction of Sisters: A Manual for Priests and Superiors,* adapted from the second German edition of Rev. A. Ehl. New York: Benziger, 1930.

Kitner, Glen D. *The Maryknoll Fathers*. New York: World, 1961.

Lane, Raymond F., M.M. *The Early Days of Maryknoll*. New York: McKay, 1951.

LaServiere, J. de, S.J. *Histoire de La Mission du Kiang-nan: Jesuites de la Province de France (Paris), 1840–1899*, vol. 1. *Jusqu'a l'etablissement d'un Vicaire apostolique jesuite (1840–1856)*. Shanghai: Catholic Mission Press, [1914?].

Latourette, Kenneth S. *A History of Christian Missions in China*. Taipei: Ch'eng Wen Publishing Co., 1970 [originally published in New York by Macmillan, 1929).

Lazaristes du Peit'ang (Peiping). *Les Missions de Chine: Treizieme Annee (1935–36)*. Shanghai: La Procure des Lazaristes, 1937.

Legrand, Francis Xavier. *The Intellectual Apostolate in China*. Hong Kong: Catholic Truth Society, 1949.

Liu, William T. and Pallone, Nathaniel J., eds. *Catholics/U.S.A.: Perspectives on Social Change*. New York: Wiley, 1970.

Lord, Daniel A. "Forward America." *Catholic Missions* 6 (Oct. 1929).

McAvoy, Thomas T. "Americanism: Fact and Fiction." *Catholic Historical Review* 31 (July 1945).

———. *Roman Catholicism and the American Way of Life*. Notre Dame, Ind.: University of Notre Dame Press, 1960.

McDonald, Raphael, O.F.M. "Prefecture Apostolic of Shasi." M.A. thesis, St. Bonaventure University, 1945.

Maguire, Theophane, C.P. *Hunan Harvest*. Privately printed, ca. 1945.

M. Marcelline, Sr. *Sisters Carry the Gospel*. Maryknoll, N.Y.: Maryknoll Publications, n.d.

Mary Just, Sr. *China—1925: A Mission Investigation*. Cincinnati, Ohio: Catholic Students Mission Crusade, 1925.

Miklas, Sebastian F., O.F.M., Cap., ed. *Franciscan View of Missiology*. Washington, D.C.: Franciscan Educational Conference, 1946.

Moore, John Ferguson. *Will America Become Catholic?* New York: Harper, 1931.

Morton, Marilyn, et al., eds. *East Asian Jesuit Secretariat Conference, Hong Kong, April 16–20, 1968*. New York: Jesuit Missions, 1968.

O'Brien, David. "American Catholicism and American Religion." *Journal of the American Academy of Religion* 40:1 (March 1972).

[O'Farrell, John J., S.J.] *A Guide to Catholic Shanghai*. T'ou-se-wei: T'ou-se-wei Press, 1937.

Official Catholic Directory. New York: P. J. Kenedy and Sons, annual.

Papal Pronouncements on the Political Order. Compiled and edited by J. Powers, C.S.V. Westminster. Md.: Newman Press, 1952.

Paul, Harry W. *The Second Ralliement: The Rapprochement Between Church and State in France in the Twentieth Century.* Washington, D.C.: Catholic University of America Press, 1967.

Pfister, Louis, S.J. *Notices Biographiques Sur les Jesuites de L'Ancien Mission de Chine, 1552–1773,* vol. 2. *XVIIIe Siècle.* Shanghai: Imprimerie de la Mission Catholique, 1934.

Powers, George C., M.M. *The Maryknoll Movement.* Maryknoll, N.Y.: Maryknoll, 1926.

Prud'homme, J.-B., S.J. "Missions Catholiques en Chine," 2d ed. (Jan. 1936). Map.

Reilly, Terence, O.P. "Mission to Kienning-fu,I" *Dominicana* 42:4 (Dec. 1957).

Ryan, Joseph P., M.M. "The American Contribution to the Catholic Missionary Effort in China in the Twentieth Century." *Catholic Historical Review* 31 (1945).

Schick, Julius M., C.M. "Diplomatic Correspondence Concerning the Chinese Missions of the American Vincentians, 1929-1934." M.A. thesis, Catholic University of America, 1951.

Schintz, Mary Ann. "An Investigation of the Modernizing Role of the Maryknoll Sisters in China." Ph.D. dissertation, University of Wisconsin-Madison, 1978.

Schmalz, Norbert, O.F.M., and Pfeilschifter, Boniface, O.F.M., *Shen Fu's Story: The Memoirs of Two Missionaries in the China of Yesteryear.* Chicago: Franciscan Herald Press, 1966.

Sharkey, Sr. Mary Agnes. *The New Jersey Sisters of Charity,* vol. 2. *Mother Mary Xavier Mehegan: The Story of Seventy-Five Years, 1859–1933.* New York: Longmans, Green & Co., 1933.

———. *The New Jersey Sisters of Charity,* vol. 3. *Our Missions, 1859–1933.* New York: Longmans, Green & Co., 1933.

Sheridan, Sr. Mary Imelda, M.M. "A Brief History of the South China Region." [Maryknoll, N.Y.?], n.d.

The Sign, Mission Department, ed. *Eyes East: On Chinese Pathways With the Passionist Missionaries.* Union City, N.J., n.d.

Society for the Propagation of the Faith, U.S. *The Mission Apostolate, a study of the mission activity of the Roman Catholic Church and the story of various mission-aid organizations in the United States.*

Stover, Leon E. *The Cultural Ecology of Chinese Civilization.* New York: New American Library, 1968.

Teng, S.Y. *The Taiping Rebellion and the Western Powers.* Oxford: Clarendon Press, 1971.

Two Encyclicals on the Foreign Missions. New York: America Press, 1944.

Unsworth, Sister Virginia F., D.C., "American Catholic Missions and Communist China, 1945–1953." Ph.D. dissertation, New York University, 1977.

Westhoven, William. "Convent Station in China," in Mission Department, *The Sign,* eds., *Eyes East: On Chinese Pathways With the Passionist Missionaries.* Union City, N.J., n.d.

Wright, Arthur F. *Buddhism in Chinese History.* New York: Atheneum, 1968.

Yang, C.K. *Religion in Chinese Society.* Berkeley and Los Angeles: University of California Press, 1967.

Index